Sebring

Nazarene

Life in a Traveling Parsonage

The Story of Paul Martin

As told by
Michael Martin
in collaboration with
T. E. Martin

Beacon Hill Press of Kansas City
Kansas City, Missouri

Dedication

To Mrs. Paul R. Martin

Contents

Foreword

Paul Martin was an original. There never has been and never will be another. This makes him a very special person to the thousands of us who knew and loved him.

He was, and is, widely known and respected. His love and laughter made him unforgettable. A modern-day "Uncle Bud," his colorful word pictures made truth come alive.

No preacher in our time touched the heartstrings of both the young and old like "Brother Paul." No evangelist in our church influenced more people to kneel at the Cross.

May this book of personal recollections bring back happy memories and deepen the commitment of all who read it to meet Paul again and share his love and laughter eternally.

EUGENE L. STOWE

Preface

When it comes to summarizing the life of someone as continuously active as Paul Martin, not even a son and a brother can have the last word! Therefore, the authors wish to say that this biography is in no way complete. A detailed description of every aspect of Paul Martin's life and career would be difficult to compile—due to the great diversity of activities in which he was engaged—and would not really serve the present purpose, which is to highlight the main events of that life and briefly describe his special talents and the ways they were used in the service of his church and the work of the Lord. Anecdotes have been chosen which hopefully reveal important sides of his character and his work, but every reader who knew him will have his own special memories. Since Paul Martin was one of the most spontaneous humorists the church ever had, he left behind him literally thousands of quotable lines and stories, only a handful of which have found their way into this book.

Nor have the authors attempted to assess Paul Martin's general place in the church or its history. Church historians of the future will be more able to judge his importance in this respect. We have confined ourselves to describing the man as we remember him and the effect his life and ministry had on the people who knew and heard him.

We have been immeasurably helped by a number of people who have given us information and memories. First of all, we would like to thank Mrs. Paul R. Martin for her help, suggestions, and information throughout the writing of the book; it is no exaggeration to say that the work could not have been completed without her invaluable contribution. Other relatives of Paul have been most helpful in supplying us with facts, anecdotes, and photographs, among them: Mrs. Leora Sharp, Mrs. Mary McKenna, and Mr. and Mrs. Ronn Pineo. We would also like to thank, in alphabetical order, the following people who contributed generously to the final work: James Blandin, Mrs. Frank A. Cooper, Dr. George Coulter, Ruby Fong, Dr. Don J. Gibson, Frank Jow, Dr. Edward Lawlor, Stanley Louie, Paul Miller, Dr. Leslie Parrott, Dr. H. T. Reza, Paul Skiles, Dr. Willis Snowbarger, Dr. Eugene L. Stowe, Leo Waldron, and Dr. E. E. Zachary.

Special thanks should be given to M. A. (Bud) Lunn and Dr. Fred Parker for their advice during the writing and completion of the manuscript.

Finally, it would be impossible to list all those who, by their association with the Martin family, added to this effort through their conversations, recollections, and fellowship over the years. Nor were we able, given the limited time, to contact everyone. Therefore, we would like to extend our appreciation to all those people who, though not mentioned directly, were invaluable contributors both to the life and the life story of Paul Martin.

MICHAEL MARTIN
T. E. MARTIN

1

A Summer Evening at Camp Meeting

It is 7:00 or 7:30 on a Saturday evening, somewhere in the Midwest, near the close of a week-long camp meeting. The air has cooled a bit from the hot, humid day. Under the tent hundreds of people have assembled. Two or three gospel songs have been sung; the announcements have been given; the offering taken; the special music presented. The speaker of the evening has been introduced, and everyone is quiet—some from anticipation, others from slight weariness, for the service has already lasted close to an hour. A middle-aged man, about 5 feet 9 inches tall, with slightly thinning, greyish hair, a rounded face, a stout figure, dressed in a business suit, and holding a Bible, approaches the pulpit.

"Every now and then I'm with an evangelist who says, 'People are always asking me to give my life story.' and so he does. But no one asks me."

A slight chuckle ripples through the crowd. Is he being serious?

"But I give it anyway!" Now more laughter.

"After all, it's almost impossible to be a full-time evangelist and not have a life story. But I am somewhat limited. I've never been in jail, except to preach the gospel. I did not come from Texas, nor was I born in a log cabin, nor did I build a log cabin in which anyone else was born. But I've got a life story. And whether you appreciate the fact or not, you are going to be afflicted with it!"

The audience is warming up to him. The casual approach, the self-mockery—a strange way to start a sermon, and yet effective. Some put down the books they were planning to read through the hour. Some of the children look up from their pencils and papers.

"Someone said to me, 'Oh, I know, Brother Martin, you used to be a TV wrestler.' But I never was. I've looked like this all my life! Someone else said, 'You must have been an athlete.' But you know better than that—you who've been out on the ball field. I had to quit playing football, because I couldn't see the ball when I could kick it, and couldn't kick it when I could see it, and under those circumstances—"

Almost everyone is laughing now. The teenagers and pastors who have played sports with him at the recreation hours during the week know what he is talking about. The few who haven't paid attention so far look up to see just what kind of shape this preacher really has!

Seriousness and humor alternate faster than anyone can keep up with or can take in. "But seriously, I owe a lot to the Church of the Nazarene. I got a letter from my district superintendent recently saying, 'Your home mission pledge is due now.' And word from the treasurer of our parsonage fund says, 'Now your pledge can be sent, Brother Martin.' As I said, I owe a lot to the Church of the Nazarene—probably more than I'll be able to pay!" Now serious again: "But all I know is the church. Don't feel sorry for me; I was born in a Nazarene parsonage. The reason was that Mother was at home at the time—

14

had she been in church, I would have been born in the church!"

By now the audience is completely with him. He has already given them more entertainment than they have had on many an eveing.

A scripture from Philippians follows, ending, "I know both how to be abased, and I know how to abound . . ."; and now, with emphasis, *"I can do all things through Christ which strengtheneth me"* (4:12-13). "Dear Jesus," he suddenly prays, "as we give a simple testimony, not of our own cleverness but of the grace of God, as we try to tell this crowd how wonderful it is to be raised in a Christian home, how good it is to be a Christian, help us, we pray, to make it worthwhile, and we shall give Thee all the praise. Amen.

"June the 10th, nineteen hundred and—none of your business; I was born in a Nazarene parsonage!"

Amusing, outrageous, and sobering incidents are described. Typical of them, the following shows well the influence of a Christian home upon this speaker:

> My mother was born in southwest Indiana. She believed that everything that wiggled was wrong— never asked any questions. Her convictions were strong; and when she married Father, who was converted in the YMCA, she had her problems. One day Father bought us a pair of boxing gloves. Mother gave him a message on the world, the flesh, and the devil. She said it didn't look right. Father, well, he didn't know. He said, "I'm sorry; I didn't think of it. You know, I never used gloves until after I was saved. Before that I used my bare knuckles and brass knuckles, and the gloves were a kind of symbol of my conversion."
>
> Mother decided it was all right. For Mother not only loved the Lord, but she loved my father. Then she said to us, "Now, boys, don't ever use them on any of the laymen's children." For Mother was not only genuinely spiritual but genuinely political. She could see a no vote a mile away. And Mother never

15

used the gloves, not even to take a hot pan out of the oven.

One Saturday we were boxing; Father was with us. In the midst of the fray a black eye began to swell out on Father. I giggled way down deep. I said, "He doesn't look much like a holiness preacher now!" Father went to the prime minister of the home. She took the gloves off and then gave him a sermon on the appearance of evil. Mother was an ordained elder, ordained by Dr. Goodwin, recommended by Dr. Miller. She could preach at the drop of a hat or the sight of a black eye; it made no difference.

She said, "I guess I'll have to preach Sunday."

Father replied, "No, I'll preach."

She answered, "No, I'll preach."

Finally, Father pulled rank on Mother and declared, "I've got a message, and I'll preach."

Mother said, "All right; and if you get in the brush, I'll shout you through!"

The next day I brought to church eight neighborhood boys who had never been there before. I said, "Dad has a black eye and is going to preach—you don't want to miss it!" They were there! Father came in, his black eye shining. The saints began to whisper; some checked Mother to see if she had any marks of the fray. Others looked at us.

Father didn't apologize or make any excuses. He stood at the pulpit until the smiling was over, and said, "My text for the morning is, 'Follow peace with all men, and holiness, without which no man shall see the Lord' (Heb. 12:14)." And I think they learned that the way of peace was the best way.

But sitting down in the crowd, this boy grew by leaps and bounds; and I've said it a million times, "O Lord, make me a man like my dad, wise and strong. I know You can!" Believe me, friend, good religion and pleasure and joy go along together. It may take a little time, Dad. It may take a little time, Mother. It may need a bit of sacrifice, friends. But along the way of life, you may find that an hour spent with a boy at play may give you a chance to spend a moment with him in prayer. If you play a little, you may pray a little.

16

And there can be a strain of love that flows through the home where God is felt, until the youngsters cannot but remember that God was there.

And so, amid bursts of laughter and sudden moments of quiet, Paul Martin tells them his story of "Life in a Nazarene Parsonage." He describes his early years as a pastor's son, the days of fun and joy, the frustrations, the embarrassments, the answers to prayer, and the victories over suffering and death. It is a story he told to hundreds of audiences, from coast to coast, during his many years of ministry. The purpose of this book is to fill out that life story, which in the sermon focused on those earlier years. It will reveal that days of joy, dedication, salvation, and victory continued to follow him throughout his life and career.

2

Paul's Parents—
Holiness Preachers

One day, in Chippewa Falls, Wis., shortly after the turn of the century, a tall, rough, grey-eyed young man, one-eighth Chippewa Indian, was working with a logging team in a canoe trying to break up a log jam just above the falls. The work was dangerous at best, but the two men guiding the canoe were drunk. The crew was successful in dislodging the logs, but they misjudged the distances. Before there was time to escape, the logs, the canoe, and all the men went over the falls together. Most were drowned in the turbulent water, but the young man was fortunate. He drifted downstream, fighting the current, and finally made it to the bank. He pulled himself out of the water far enough to be able to breathe, but he was too exhausted to drag himself to safety.

As he lay there, an older woodsman emerged from the forest. He had seen the terrible accident from a distance. As he helped the young man out of the water, he said, "You should be grateful to be alive, for many have drowned." Then he began to speak to him about Christ and about his soul.

The young man swore angrily, and the older man

disappeared into the woods. Yet this message stayed with the young logger. Later, when he came to know Christ, he attempted to look up this witness to Christ's saving power; for, in a sense, this was the first real encounter with the Christian message that anyone in the Martin family had had. The young man was Edward Everett Martin, Paul Martin's father.

He was a restless person in those days. He played some football with Jim Thorpe at the Haskell Institute, a school for Indians in Lawrence, Kans.; but he ran away after a few months to join the army. He was sent to Fort Wadsworth, N.Y. There he came to know Arthur Moseley, YMCA secretary and a strong Christian. It was under his preaching and influence that Edward Everett gave his heart to Jesus Christ. He met and married Arletta Holston in 1909. She was a Methodist deaconess from Indiana who had been asked by Moseley to assist in the spiritual part of his program at Fort Wadsworth. They were married in a YMCA chapel. As Paul often related in his sermon, the ceremony turned into an evangelistic service, in which several young servicemen sought the Lord.

Arletta Holston had been converted at age 9. She had an indomitable will. She could be thought of as a woman truly liberated by the Christian gospel. Against her father's wishes, she sought and found the sanctifying power of the Holy Spirit at age 16. And against the equally strong prejudices of society at that time, she became a minister, accepting Arthur Moseley's offer at age 23.

When Edward was discharged at the end of his enlistment period, he wanted to spend his life as a street preacher. He was an athlete who enjoyed football, handball, and boxing, which is probably why he enjoyed the milieu of confrontation that preaching on the street afforded. Arthur Moseley admired Edward's fervor but also knew his limitations. Edward Martin had not even finished high school.

Possibly it was his regret at having run away from school, halting his educational development, that contributed to his lifetime of study. Edward finished his high school and college piecemeal while pastoring nearby churches and raising a family of two girls and three boys. He obtained his Master of Arts degree in pastoral counseling from Boston University when he was 62 years of age!

Sensing this determination about him, Moseley urged Edward to consider the pastoral ministry. Since Moseley and Arletta were both Methodists, that denomination seemed the most logical for the recently converted soldier. But there was much about Methodism that they did not like. They were "holiness Methodists," and the doctrine of entire sanctification was being attacked both by direct refutation and political isolation. A holiness preacher found himself opposed or mocked and frequently shunted to hostile churches by the hierarchy.

In 1909 when Edward and Arletta were needing to make a decision concerning their church affiliation, Moseley read of a new holiness denomination called the Church of the Nazarene which had been founded in Pilot Point, Tex., in October of 1908. He advised Edward to get into it at the start. He told him that he felt such a church was timely and would grow. "They will need preachers rapidly," he told my father, "for there are many holiness people looking for such a fellowship. In spite of your limited education, you have a good chance to get in on the ground floor and grow with the church."

A letter to Dr. Phineas F. Bresee, the founding general superintendent, was referred to District Superintendent Hoople in New York. Almost before they were ready, Edward and Arletta had been appointed to the

Church of the Nazarene in Cliftondale, Mass.

One year in Cliftondale brought their child, Leora, into their parsonage and Edward's ordination by Dr. Bresee. But it also convinced the new preacher that he had much to learn. So after a year of trying his hand at pastoring, he accepted the position of associate pastor with Rev. A. B. Riggs at Lowell, Mass. For three years he worked and learned under one of the ablest Nazarene ministers in New England. During these three years his family grew to three children with the birth of Theodore Edward and Everett Riggs. Everett was named for his father and his much-loved mentor.

It was after more than four years of marriage and learning the ropes of pastoral ministry that Edward Martin grew restless to be on his own. He confided his concern to Dr. Bresee one day in Lowell. The general superin-

Martin family picture, 1931, Nampa, Ida. *Front row,* left to right: Mrs. E. E. Martin, Paul; *Back row,* Mary, Ted, Rev. E. E. Martin, Everett, and Leora.

21

tendent told him that he had just come from answering a request for help in developing a new work in western Canada. A church had been organized in Calgary, Alberta, two years before, and he offered young Martin the challenge of going there to pastor the church and evangelize in the western area of that great country. In 1913, just before the outbreak of World War I, the Martin family moved to Canada to establish a holiness witness on the western prairies. This they did by strengthening the new church in Calgary, by evangelizing and laying the foundation for the church at Drumheller, and by pastoring the church at Claresholm, while adding to the list of children Paul La Rouche*—born June 10, 1915—and Mary Evelyn. Ted (Theodore) had been told that he would have a second baby brother, and he wondered if the baby was in the black bag the doctor carried into the house!

So Paul Martin was indeed a child of the church—the son of two holiness, Nazarene ministers. He was born in a parsonage, and, in fact, spent all his life in one, if the apartments he rented from his preaching income could be called parsonages. He grew up with the influence of holiness and the sanctified life ingrained into the home. From his father he learned of Christ's ability to change lives completely—to give them a new direction, a new purpose. From his mother, he learned about the true dedication of a Christian life, including the determination to serve, to fulfill one's calling, no matter what the obstacles.

-----

*There is some disagreement about Paul's second name. It was his grandmother Martin's maiden name. Her family was French-Indian. The spelling is the controversy. There is no French word *Rouche*. There is a word *la ruche* which means "beehive" and seems appropriate to Paul. At any rate he later dropped the article *la* and changed the spelling to "Rush," which also became appropriate as he in adult life gave himself to the demanding work of preaching and evangelizing. He was indeed Paul RUSH Martin.

3

Paul's Early Years—
His Bout with Polio

Paul's life really became definitive for his two brothers and two sisters because of an event in the sagebrush-covered hills to the east of Mountain Home, Ida., about 60 miles from Nampa. The Martin family had moved to Mountain Home in the summer of 1918 to pastor the church there while Rev. Martin attended Northwest Nazarene Academy.

Ted Martin recalls: "Many of the things I think I remember belong to the borderland of memory and fantasy and probably are the results of the stories we have told each other about those days. Quite clear in my memory, however, was the afternoon we were some distance from the house under the direction of my older sister, Leora, who usually was put in command when Mother was busy or away from the house.

"It was late in the afternoon and we had been ordered by our older sister to head for home. Paul, about three years old, was stumbling and falling. We had to drag him because he claimed he could not stand up or walk. He was right. After some tense hours at home, we were informed that our youngest brother was the victim of infantile paralysis. He then became the center of the family concern and remained so for some time. He grew worse rather than better. He lost the use of his legs and arms. He lay for days with a fever. Finally Mother found it nearly impossible to feed him. He could hardly swallow and we feared his throat was paralyzed."

Mrs. Martin, in her book *Miracles in White,* says, "For two weeks we cared for him. I could visualize my child with a twisted body, in braces, and an invalid for life. But in the early hours of the morning, God whispered to my heart, 'Nothing is impossible to Me.'"

"The family altar which convened daily in our home centered on Paul and his battle for life," continues Ted. "One day, years before the world learned of Sister Kenny and her massage treatment of polio victims, Mother announced she felt deeply impressed to treat Paul by wrapping his arms and legs with warm towels and massaging them. 'Deeply impressed' was her term for the conviction that God had spoken. She conferred with the doctor, who felt it could do no harm. And so the treatment began. After the fever had subsided, all of us were conscripted to participate. And we were glad to do it. Paul had become for all of us the symbol of our determination to survive. Against his protest that we were too rough, which I'll admit in my case may have had some justification, we persevered."

Leora Sharp, Paul's older sister, says, "After Mother had massaged Paul, she would set him on the kitchen table and swing his legs. Then she would say, 'Look, Paul, your legs will swing. Now you swing them.' How we all rejoiced when we finally saw him make a very small movement! Gradually he was able to use his limbs again. For about four years, he would swing each leg out to the side as he brought it forward to take a step, but he never wore braces or used crutches."

Ted continues: "He had to learn to walk all over again. It was interesting to see a three-year-old push around the chair and haltingly try to keep up by an unsteady walk. Every bit of progress brought joy to him and cheers from us. We conspired to keep him happy. If he did anything, we applauded. We told him jokes, acted out stories, and did everything we could think of to entertain him. And soon he learned the joy of entertaining. It was no longer necessary to do things to amuse him. He amused us. If at first we overdid our applause, soon he really was the life of the party (and life in the Martin home was a party, as he later tells in his *Life in a Nazarene Parsonage*). If he ever knew, he never mentioned how much he and his miraculous recovery from polio initiated a camaraderie that characterized the family. It never ceased. Even when we were grown and had homes of our own, family get-togethers which were too few were always hilarious.

"As I look back at it now, I realize that in those difficult days God saved our brother from dying or being a cripple, and also He gave us a warmth of love and fun that was worth more than anything good health or money could have given. We learned the reality of prayer, the power of love, and the wealth of laughter."

In *Miracles in White* Mrs. Martin ends her section on this event by saying, "Today one would not know from his appearance that the boy had ever been afflicted with infantile paralysis. The disease left him with a trembling which will perhaps follow him through life unless God sees fit to remove that also. The Lord has done great things for the lad already. Praise His name!"

Paul grew up in his father's pastorates—at Meridian, Ida.; Ontario, Ore.; Lowell and Worcester, Mass.; and Nampa, Ida., where he finished high school and entered Northwest Nazarene College. His sense of humor showed

25

itself early. Mary McKenna, Paul's younger sister, recalls that in high school he did well in his readings and speaking, won honors and awards, and gave talks in small communities around Nampa. If he forgot part of a speech, he could ad lib so effectively that many could not distinguish between the prepared and the improvised. And it got so that, because of the gift of spontaneous humor, the ad lib parts were liked as much or more than the original.

His unpredictable humor and lightheartedness could erupt at any time. Mary McKenna relates that their brother Everett was taking an interior decorating class. He would come home and demonstrate how the furniture in the parsonage should be placed, according to the principles learned in the class. The family grew a bit tired of all these rearrangements and suggestions on artistic improvement. One day, when the rest of the family came home, they found that Paul had turned all the chairs and tables upside down. He then proceeded to give the family a lecture on this latest form of interior decorating, the fashionable, modern way of decorating a home.

Paul's quick mind showed itself early. When he started school, the teachers decided to skip him to the second grade. But he was still too advanced, so after about a week he was put into the third grade. His mother's theory about his brightness was that, while his body was paralyzed with polio, his brain grew twice as fast! When Paul was in the seventh grade, the school wanted to promote him again to the eighth, but the parents felt that since he was two grades ahead already, the move might be difficult socially.

Other facts from high school and college years show a personality destined for some sort of public life: member of the high school debate team, snapshot editor of the yearbook at Northwest Nazarene College, sergeant of arms of the associated student body at NNC, and even a cheerleader for one year at Nampa.

In the summer between school terms, while working in the onion fields around Nampa, Paul announced to his fellow workers, "I am going to go with Monica Chandler!" The others had some reason to be surprised, for no two people had more different backgrounds than Paul and Monica. She was the daughter of a prominent physician and surgeon in northwestern Washington State, in the Mukilteo-Everett area. Her background was of course well-to-do and refined; Paul, on the other hand, was far from well-off, and his manners and refinement left a lot to be desired at that time.

On his first date, she let him know that he wasn't all she had in mind—his appearance, especially, wasn't all she expected. Paul must have already been very interested in her, for he took up the challenge. He really prepared for his second date. He plastered his hair down with so much heavy hair oil and conditioner that it was dripping down his collar when he met Monica. Also, he liberally applied some cologne his sister had given him, but in the process he dropped the bottle, which broke on the floor. Worried that he didn't smell good enough, he bent down and sat in the puddle of cologne! He must have looked and smelled unbelievably sweet that evening!

But these were signs of real interest and love. Leora Sharp says, "Paul had a lot of girl friends during his high school and college years. As his older sister, I watched with interest while he seemed to go from one girl to another with an air of indifference as each girl strove to become special to him. Then one day he met Monica Chandler. There was a sudden change. He began to comb his hair carefully and to dress with pride. I could hardly believe what I was seeing. When I asked him what had happened, he said simply, 'Monica likes me this way.' And that's the way it was from that time on."

27

While in college, they decided to get married. In those days it was against the rules to marry during the school year, so they were married by Paul's parents in a home in a nearby town. Meanwhile, they had arranged to move to Mukilteo, Wash., Monica's hometown. There Paul continued his education at Seattle Pacific College and the University of Washington. After six months, at the end of the school year, Paul's father, who was then district superintendent of the North Pacific District, had arranged for Paul to pastor the little Nazarene church in Mukilteo. By age 19, he was a pastor and husband—an early age to take on such responsibilities. Ted says, "For us, Paul's early entrance into the serious task of ministry and home-making were traumatic; we thought of it as both tragic and hopeful—tragic because in depression times he had a home before he had a dime to call his own, hopeful because he married one of the finest and most talented girls we ever knew. We often said that if Paul ever makes it, it will be because of Monica."

And so the story must move from his father's parsonage to his own.

4

"And a Little Child Shall Lead Them"

Paul's first pastorate in Mukilteo was a period of experiment, of trial and error, with a healthy portion of errors! Years later he still remembered his welcoming reception in this, his first church. The master of ceremonies chose as his theme the passage from Isa. 11:6: "and a little child shall lead them." For a 19-year-old

Paul, at 19 years of age.

still in college the scripture must have seemed embarrassingly appropriate.

It was with great enthusiasm that the young Martin family prepared for this first pastorate. In fact, instead of waiting discreetly for the departing pastor and family to move out before arriving on the scene, Paul and Monica stood at the parsonage gate and waved them away, eagerly waiting for them to turn the corner so that they could move into their first home together.

The parsonage had a beautifully laid-out garden of vegetables, which were almost ready to use. Paul and Monica's first and last vegetable gardening experience was completed that first day. Assuming the vegetables were weeds, they pulled them all up and tossed them into the trash. The barren garden was some surprise to the members as they walked by the following Sunday.

During the first revival meeting there, Paul made a four-mile drive each night to pick up six ladies who were not members of the church but were interested in it. They were all successful and affluent—desirable prospects for the small, growing church. The first lady to be picked up was Mrs. Wade. She was waiting on her doorstep the first night and waved as Paul's car approached. He waved back and drove right on by, picking up the others and returning to the meeting. The second night, Mrs. Wade was out by her gate waving frantically at Paul as he approached. He smiled, waved back, and drove on by again. The third night, Mrs. Wade stood in the middle of the highway, waving both hands; and this time Paul did stop —to keep from hitting her! But she forgave him and, along with the other ladies, eventually joined the church.

But he began to learn quickly, as he always did. Right away he realized the importance of calling, of visitation. He and Monica called on every member the first two weeks. And he learned to appreciate and take into account other people's strong feelings and prejudices.

One especially amusing story concerns Monica's grandfather, Jefferson Smith, father of the first NYPS president in the Nazarene church, Donnell J. Smith. Jefferson Smith lived just across the street from the parsonage. He was an early riser and was convinced that all successful young ministers should be early risers also. Paul soon solved that problem. Every morning, at 6 a.m., he built a fire in the kitchen stove so that Grandfather Smith could see the smoke rising from the chimney. Then he went back to bed and slept until 8:30 or 9:00! So both were satisfied.

The first pastorate is exhausting physically and emotionally for many ministers. Paul seems to have been affected the same way. Once, in prayer meeting, the congregation was on its knees in prayer. Paul had been asking various people to pray. But an unusually long silence occurred between the last prayer and the traditional closing prayer by the pastor. Paul's mother-in-law was quick to sense the problem, and she quietly crept over to his pew and woke him up!

During the Mukilteo pastorate, Paul came to know well a man who was a formative influence on his adult life—his father-in-law, Dr. Claude Chandler. He was the most prominent doctor in Mukilteo throughout his life. A man of great dedication and dignity, he is still talked about and remembered with love by the people of Mukilteo old enough to have been his friend or patient. His sense of responsibility; his cautious, yet warm and friendly, manner; and his great capacity for hard work were just the right influence for Paul at this impressionable age. He helped to guide the young minister towards a keener sense of responsibility and dedication in his own area. And he was always there to help the young couple financially, during those depression years.

31

Dr. Chandler developed an angina condition at the early age of 50. Instead of slowing down, he worked just as hard or harder, undoubtedly shortening his life. During the last six months, he was in great pain but continued his work without interruption. (He treated his last patient on Saturday night before he died on Monday.) It is an interesting parallel to Paul, who later in his 50s developed this same form of heart disease and who also refused to slow down.

With the death of Dr. Chandler, the young couple were suddenly on their own, bereft of his companionship and his support. It was the first bereavement to hit them both. Monica remembers that this was a period when they both grew up very quickly. The worries of security, the vulnerabilities to the larger, hostile world, suddenly arose, and they had to rely on their own strengths to see them through. But Dr. Chandler's influence did not stop with his death—it acted as an inspiration and guideline throughout the lives of Paul and Monica, and was crucial to Paul's spiritual growth and ministry.

Beginning in January, 1938, after three years at Mukilteo, Paul and Monica started out as a full-time evangelistic team. Their special emphasis at this time was on children's and youth work. Those who later saw his children's services or have seen him take over a Sunday school service know how skilled and entertaining he was with children.

The first questions anyone might ask a minister starting out in full-time evangelism are "What will you do to hold the people's interest?" and, very practically, "How will you get meetings?" The last problem was partially overcome by the help of Paul's father. Since he was district superintendent of that area, he could help arrange meetings. So Paul and Monica traveled from one home mission church to the other, slowly gaining in recognition. They expanded their ministry into western Canada and the Northern California District. The second problem —attracting an audience—was more difficult, and trial and error again played its role here.

In high school Monica Chandler had had a radio program. She had a good radio voice, and the program was a success. When she and her husband became pastors of the Mukilteo church, five miles away, the station managers were receptive to a combined husband-and-wife program of a religious nature. Monica's father bought her a Vibraharp, which had come into fashion only the decade before. Paul read poetry and inspirational thoughts while Monica played. They continued doing this as an evangelistic team, and the program worked quite successfully.

What was not so successful were their attempts to sing. There will be more written about Paul Martin's "singing" in another chapter. Suffice to say here that they both had trouble carrying a tune very well. In one meeting they sang a duet, and Paul's mother was in the audience. On their way home, she was unusually quiet. Then she burst out, "Paul, don't you ever do that again! You'll drive the people away!" They took her advice and dropped that idea from their program.

Monica gave readings of her own during evangelistic meetings and also put together felt-o-grams. Elmer Gandy, a well-known artist, who worked in Yosemite Valley for many years before becoming an evangelist, painted some of these desert and mountain landscapes for Monica. They also used a color wheel, so that the pictures would change hue slowly. Paul read the poems while the felt-o-gram was being made, and he continued as Monica moved over to play the Vibraharp. The results were effective, particularly to the children and young people to whom their ministry was especially geared at that point.

His ability to win people over and his confidence in preaching and evangelizing grew quickly. Ted Martin recalls: "I invited Paul and Monica to visit my home in Connell, Wash. It was my second church, and I imagined myself to be an experienced older brother who could help a neophyte to make it. Connell was in the center of large dryland wheat farms in those days. I had first come to be known there while in college. Numbers of the young men from college at Nampa would go to the wheat fields to work in the harvest during the summer. I got Paul a job with the same farmer that I was working for. Paul and Monica came and stayed with us. Paul and I rode each day to the farm. It was a memorable month together in which I came to know my sister-in-law and to realize how much my brother had become a man. He preached in the church and the people loved him. They would say to me that I could leave anytime if my brother would take my place. They told me they would gain in the bargain.

"Paul began to feel more confident in the thoughts of evangelistic work. For one thing he found he could do an acceptable job of holding children's attention and moving them to spiritual understanding. His fame as a children's worker spread. His ministry drew the attention of larger churches and camp meetings. The story is told in California that when Paul was holding children's meetings during the same hour that Dr. H. Orton Wiley was teaching Bible study, more adults attended the children's meetings! It finally became necessary to schedule the two services at different times to guarantee a Bible study crowd."

During this time Paul and Monica held a meeting in Calgary, Alberta. Dr. Edward Lawlor, who was pastoring there, suggested to Paul that he do a "Life in a Parsonage" story. This was the beginning of a sermon that Paul preached more often than any other, from that time until

34

his death. They were always grateful to Dr. Lawlor for suggesting the idea, for it combined Paul's talent for humor with sudden shifts to the serious and poignant descriptions of the battles and victories over hardships and death.

In 1940, Paul's mother was dying of cancer. She knew it and even rejoiced in the fact that she would soon be in heaven. She had one final prayer with Paul and Monica that year. Drawing breath intermittently from an oxygen tank by the bed, she prayed, "Lord, give Paul a life of fruitful evangelism. Give him *souls,* not wealth, but *souls.*" Paul, who never became wealthy from his ministry, but who was instrumental in thousands accepting the Lord over the years, always felt that that prayer especially was answered.

5

Three Pastorates

In December of 1941, Paul and Monica were holding a meeting in Tulare, Calif. On the last Sunday there, the news broke that the Japanese had attacked Pearl Harbor. Throughout the next meeting, in San Luis Obispo, there were frequent blackouts. Blue cellophane had to be placed over the windows, and the church congregation was ordered to stay in the building during the alert (which couldn't keep Paul from slipping out the back door to see what was going on). In a few months, a far stricter gas regulation than we have had in this decade was in effect, and the evangelistic life, with its dependence on the car, was becoming impossible. Paul accepted the church in Glendale, Calif., which started his second period of pastoral ministry, comprising three churches.

Monica remembers the time in Glendale as "delightful. A new parsonage was bought for us. There was a beautiful group of people to work with who really enjoyed Paul's ministry." During this pastorate Paul did further work at Pasadena College. He became district young people's president of the Southern California District and was elected to the General NYPS Convention and to the General Assembly. His name was being mentioned more often in more places. The family has old newspaper clippings of caricatures of him advertising revivals, youth conferences, etc. He and a group of ministers sent a letter of criticism to President Roosevelt for using a mild profanity in public—rather different times from now! He was beginning to take notice of the larger world and to get involved as much as possible.

Mary McKenna mentions an experience that illustrates a lifelong characteristic of Paul. She and her husband were living in La Jolla, where he was stationed as an army medical doctor. One morning they were having breakfast with Paul and Monica at the famous Sardis Restaurant in Hollywood, which had a radio program originating from there in those days. While they were eating, Walter Brennan, a well-known actor, walked by. Paul jumped up and said, "Well, Walt, I'm glad to see you!" Brennan couldn't place Paul in his mind—not surprising, since they'd never met before—but he thought they must have met at some time or another. So, pretending, Brennan said, "Fine, and how are you?" and they chatted for a while. Dr. McKenna could hardly believe it at that time; but when people have gotten to know Paul well, the story doesn't seem surprising. He was at ease with anyone and made anyone he met feel comfortable. This quality was invaluable in all aspects of his ministry.

While pastoring in Glendale, Paul and Monica had their only child, Michael. Because of the war conditions and the large immigration into the Los Angeles area from the South and Middle West for work in the defense factories, the hospitals were overcrowded. Paul and Monica decided that for the birth of their child she should return to the Mukilteo hospital where her father had been a staff doctor and where there were private rooms with more

37

adequate facilities. Everything was planned carefully: She would leave on the 15th of November; their son would arrive on the 15th of December; Paul would fly north on the 20th of December.

But things didn't work out quite according to plan. The variable nature of birth wasn't taken into account, and Michael was born early on the 7th. Moreover, Paul's enthusiasm was underestimated. When he was phoned at 6:30 p.m. on December 7 and told he had a son, he spent the remainder of the night calling every relative, friend, and church member he could think of, including the district superintendent! The church board met before dawn the next morning and arranged for Paul to take the next plane for Seattle, gave him a four-week paid vacation, and told him to stay until the whole family could return together. They probably thought this decision was best for both the pastor and the church, if anyone was to get any sleep!

In 1946, Paul took his next pastorate in Berkeley, Calif. Berkeley was and is a beautiful town, very close to the metropolitan area of San Francisco, with its busy atmosphere and interesting cultural events. Yet, especially at that time, it was also a small, quiet university community.

The parsonage was next door to the church, at the time they arrived, and over 60 percent of the members lived in a radius of 12 to 16 blocks. Some of the older members tended to drop by the church study or parsonage daily. A few of the more discerning members of the church board said to each other, "If we are going to keep Paul Martin as pastor, we had better look for a new parsonage." In three months, the family moved to the Berkeley hills, on Euclid Avenue, high above the university. To reach the house, one had to climb 37 steps to the front door. Some of the older members complained about the difficulty of getting up the hill and climbing these steps to reach the parsonage. Paul laughingly said, "That's the general idea!"

Monica always maintained that this time was "one of the most beautiful interludes of our lives." It was a successful and happy three-year pastorate. The parsonage itself was unusually beautiful. From the large living room window, master bedroom, and Michael's nursery, they could see directly across the bay to San Francisco itself, the Golden Gate, and far out into the Pacific Ocean. And Paul was in contact with two groups of people he especially enjoyed: college students and university teachers. The young adults became one of his favorite classes and social groups. About 30 of these were students—undergraduate and graduate—of the University of California. A number of very interesting, successful, and dedicated people came from that group, among them Willis Snowbarger, now administrator at Olivet Nazarene College.

"We never cease to marvel at the key role Paul and Monica played in our lives," says Dr. Snowbarger. "The first year of my return from the service was rough in every way. I hit my stride in graduate work at the University of Oklahoma; but when we went to Berkeley, we really needed a pastor. Without other acquaintances in Berkeley, the Martins took us to their hearts. Straight preaching, socializing after church and at other times, and responding to intellectual questions, poking fun at us, believing in us—these were the means Paul and Monica employed to save a university student and his wife."

During this time Paul became district NYPS president of the Northern California District. He also was involved in the beginnings of the Lamplighters organization. The poem of this group, by Grace Noll Crowell, was one he was to quote frequently during his subsequent years

39

of pastoring and evangelism, as part of the climax of the candlelight service he became known for:

> *I shall light my lamp from faith's white spark,*
> *And through this wild storm hold it high.*
> *Perhaps across the utter dark*
> *Its light will flash against the sky*
> *Straight enough and strong enough*
> *For some lost soul, to guide him by.*

In 1950 they moved to their last pastorate in this series—Porterville, Calif. Quite a change from Berkeley! Porterville is a small town in the central valley of California, surrounded by farming land and orange groves. Like any move from city to country, or vice versa, it took some getting used to. But they were blessed with more than 100 teenagers, an active group of young married couples, and a kindly group of good Nazarenes. It proved to be a very rewarding three years.

Both of them started their radio work again. Paul had two programs: "Thoughtful Moments with Your Radio Pastor" and a children's program, "Uncle Paul's Merry-go-round." Monica had a daily radio program called "My Ladies' Matinee with Monica," which went on for two years. The latter program more than paid for the church time, and Monica was honored by the city of Porterville for her work in this area.

During the Porterville period, Paul told the story "Life in a Nazarene Parsonage" to service clubs up and down the San Joaquin Valley, from Bakersfield to Sacramento. It was a means of helping many men and their families outside the church. Some continued to call him long distance through the years, to see if he remembered to pray for them. And he could truthfully say that he had.

This "going the extra mile" to remember people in prayer, send them letters frequently (even once a day, if he felt they needed his encouragement), or visit them constantly was a characteristic of Paul. Incidences of his concern could fill a chapter in itself. Mrs. Frank A. Cooper, the prominent cattle owner in Tulare County and generous patron of Pasadena/Point Loma College over the years, knew Paul well during the Porterville days. She recalls: "He had a depth of compassion, a sense of need, and selfless giving of service to others. For 14 weeks he drove to the Tulare Hospital to pray for my sister's husband who suffered a train-truck accident. He was not a Nazarene, nor did Paul know the members of my brother-in-law's family. God answered our prayers."

Here is a biographer's intrusion about Paul's help: Much later, I was studying for my Ph.D. orals—always a trying time in a student's career. Two weeks before the orals, Dad began to send me a postcard, one a day, containing short thoughts, bits of advice to be taken or forgotten, prayers for the success of the examination. I began to look forward to these daily cards that took on the appearance of something between the relaxing conversation a person makes while he is resting during a grueling hike and a devotional for the day.

There are other cases of laymen and clergymen alike, who have been going through a great concern, burden, or serious illness, who have been the recipients of these letters and phone calls. These, by the receivers' testimony, were of great help and inspiration. More than one person, Christian or not, relative or acquaintance, adult or child, said, after Paul's death: "I've lost my best friend." The constancy of prayer and the thoughtfulness with no ulterior motive attached were primary reasons for these statements.

Paul had a spontaneous, almost reckless side to him. If he got an idea for an adventure, an eagerness to do something, it was difficult if not impossible to dissuade him,

41

never mind the advisability or even safety of the endeavor. Knowing this personality, the Lord must have given him a special portion of His protection.

Once he decided to take the Porterville Junior High School group on a trip to Death Valley. Michael was seven at the time, and it seemed like a great adventure to him, not being aware of the adult's considerations and concerns. For one thing, the bus wasn't insured for liability to cover such a trip with so many people. For another, the bus was old, the kind that Paul used to preach about as "having an engine where the pistons went down, flopped around, and came up a different hole every time. If the driver lost his way, the bus would come home by itself." But Death Valley was farther from home than flopping pistons and homing instinct could carry it: about 400 miles away over rough road and through one of the most hostile deserts in the country—or the world, for that matter. Fierce winds blew sand and rocks across the road.

Things went pretty well, until just after they had visited Scotty's castle, at the north end of Death Valley. On the way back, one tire blew. All of the kids jumped out to play in the sand dunes, while Paul was left to jack up the bus and do the changing. A few miles later, another tire blew. And then another! Finally, the entire wheel left the axle and went spinning over the hillside, while the bus sank slightly to the right. One of the members of the church had to drive 90 miles back to Ridgecrest to pick up more tires—we were all out!

But finally the intrepid group arrived at Whitney Portal, to camp and prepare for a climb up Mount Whitney the next day. They wouldn't have gotten very far in any case, for Whitney in the spring is still snow-covered; but that night a snowstorm descended into the camp, and everyone had to return to Lone Pine. The next day they returned to Porterville, to a group of very relieved parents.

42

The phone had been ringing continually at the parsonage ever since the group had left.

Paul and Monica attended the General Assembly in June of 1952. After that, they felt definitely that evangelism was meant to be Paul's lifework. He and Monica decided that when he compiled a solid six months evangelistic slate, it would be the time to announce their decision to the church. By November, 1952, calls had come in from all parts of the United States and Canada, and the six months slate was full. The church board was notified, and by the end of December, Paul Martin was once again a full-time evangelist.

At first they moved north to Mukilteo and took a small apartment near the family home. Michael went to

Paul and Monica during the first period of evangelism.

school there, and Monica was there much of the time, while Paul traveled almost continuously. Clearly, this situation had its problems if the family were to remain together. After some research and advice from other families in a similar position, they found a good correspondence school, Calvert School in Baltimore. The program, course of instruction, and subjects to be covered were sent to the parents, who then became teachers for their child. Papers and exams were sent back to Baltimore, graded, and returned to the family. The school proved to be a very good one, and Michael was almost always ahead of the work covered in the regular public school curriculum. After six months in Mukilteo, Monica and Michael joined Paul to become part of the full-time evangelistic team. This way of life was to extend over the next five years.

6

A New Challenge

One of the successes to Paul Martin's ministry was the ability to adapt his ministry, his style, his method of presentation to the changing times. He never bogged down in a certain format and remained content with it. As a youngster, I used to get bothered that Dad changed his sermons so often. If something worked well, why change it? Besides, I heard him so often, at least three times a week, that I knew every one of his sermons by memory. I liked to sit with some of the kids near the front of the church and nudge them whenever a good joke or story was coming. But then he would change it a bit, then a lot. Some sermons grew suddenly more serious; entirely serious sermons were introduced. What I didn't realize, of course, was that here was an important, indeed, a necessary and saving aspect to Dad's speaking. It was his way of keeping his message alive.

Right away he perceived, as he began this period of travel, that he must counter an image that had been growing up about him: that he was basically a children's worker and a comedian. He had to counter this image, because he was so skillful in both areas. Children always did love him; he knew how to get their attention and hold it. Through stories, puppets, tricks, building suspense, perfect timing, he usually, by the end of a meeting, had every child riding on "Uncle Paul's Merry-go-round." And humor was almost as natural to him as eating, which was natural enough! He could thaw almost any audience; they might resist for a while, but eventually they would succumb to this satirical, at times almost irreverent, happy voice.

But he was keenly aware that more would be needed and expected of him for a serious, adult ministry. He began to downplay the Captain Kangaroo image, relegate his children's work to the Sunday school, and to mix his humor with serious and sobering observations. Those who remember the Paul Martin of "Life in a Nazarene Parsonage" probably also remember the Paul Martin of "How Far Are We from Home?" or "He That Being Often Reproved."

He sought out and accepted whenever possible the more demanding and serious tasks of evangelism. I remember his pleasure when he was invited for a camp meeting in the early 50s. He was eager to establish a reputation as a serious camp meeting speaker. I remember asking Mother what a camp meeting was, and why did Father consider it so important, and she explained it to me. Speaking at camp was building a new and important aspect of his ministry.

He did indeed succeed in becoming a powerfully serious preacher, a side that went along with, and was an effective foil to, his humor. Nor did his ministry stay with children alone. The change had to come naturally, or it would never have succeeded.

If I may be permitted an observation here: It seems to me that both comedy and children are often underrated. Our best humorists often perceived the dark side of life, its tragic side, very well. Mark Twain, whom Father loved to read and recite, is a perfect example; those who are not familiar with this great author's total work are often quite startled when they come across a brutally honest, unflinching look at tragedy and despair. But if anything, the humor grew out of these perceptions, and a testimony to the survival of the human spirit can be seen in this growth. In a much different, yet related, way it was the same with Father.

Second, those who have understood children well have understood a good deal about human nature. They have seen the adult side of the child and, conversely, are often sensitive to the child side of the adult. A great philosopher once said, "A man's maturity . . . consists in having found again the seriousness he had as a child, at play." Father's ability to entertain and move children was related to his later ability to influence and guide in the adult world. One gift is essential for both: a keen understanding of human nature.

Monica saw these and other changes as being necessary. She felt that Paul's ministry should take precedence over the musical side of their work or the children's meeting elements that had dominated before. She sold the Vibraharp for this reason—to avoid the temptation to return to the older style. In those first years of return to evangelism, she continued for a while to do the felt-o-grams and puppet shows for the children's services, but eventually phased those out as well. She continued to give readings for Sunday school and NYPS meetings throughout this time.

Perhaps the biggest challenge in this new period of evangelism was the extension of their world of travel. Before his pastorates Paul had been known primarily on the West Coast and in western Canada. Now he accepted meetings in all parts of the country. The challenge of relating to, of being accepted by, people of strikingly different backgrounds—and ultimately of being a messenger of God to them—is greater than many realize. Many ministers and speakers never extend beyond a fairly limited geographical and cultural area; they stay among a people who "understand their language," share certain prejudices, enjoy the same rhetorical customs. The challenge of Paul Martin at this point was to travel throughout one of the most complex, culturally complicated countries in the world, and to minister equally well in its various contrasting areas.

This took a while to do. At first he was accepted in certain areas more than others. He was not strict enough for some, not formal enough for others. He quickly discovered that humor is a very complicated matter, dividing people as much as bringing them together. One can imagine each meeting as a kind of learning experience for him; if something didn't work one time, change it a bit. An illustration might be successful one place and not in another. The important thing, always, was the ability to change. Eventually he was well accepted in almost every region.

7

The Traveling Parsonage

—Days of Fun, Adventure, and Prayer on the Road

Most people's contact with an evangelist lasts from the time he steps onto the platform to the time he finishes speaking. Those who went to gatherings organized by Paul Martin, including men's breakfasts, women's coffee-break prayer meetings, women's luncheons, morning services, children's Sunday school meetings; or those who had him for dinner during the revival or were visited by him and the pastor, got to know him much better than this. But for most, their acquaintance started and ended with the revival week, perhaps to resume if he were called back. What was an evangelist's life like before and after—in other words, what was the day-to-day routine, the continuity that gave flesh and blood to this public image? I recall several things about life in the "traveling parsonage."

I traveled with my father and mother from age 9 to 13. In those years, we had no fixed home; my grandmother's home in Mukilteo, Wash., was the closest thing to that. We would come back there once every couple of months—sometimes we were away as long as half a year.

Otherwise, our home was wherever we were that week, from one coast to the other. Father often used an illustration about a little girl who is standing in the street, watching her home go up in flames. Someone says to her: "How terrible, you've lost your home." "Oh, no," says the child, "we just don't have a house to put it in." Hardly could a story be more applicable to our life at that time. The house?—well, that was the motel that week, the pastor's home, or the guest room of a family in the church, who had generously offered to keep us. Our *home* was the close bond between the three of us.

When he first started his full-time travels, Dad had not yet developed the ability to arrange his meetings by geographical section in a way that would minimize travel. (Actually, he never was very good at this technique; so in every year's slate there were always a number of 1,200-mile trips to be completed in two days or so.) Many of my memories of that time involve travel, from one coast to the other, from the Gulf straight north to a meeting in Canada. Very often he and my mother paired off in driving all night and through most of the next day. Cars were fairly large then, and getting larger—spacious enough to accommodate the three of us, including one active youngster, without too much trouble.

In fact, it was a "house" of sorts. The bedroom was the backseat, long enough in those days for me or even my parents to stretch out. Between the backseat and the front was luggage—mountains of it—forming a kind of wall or partition, giving the sleeper some feeling of privacy. The front seat was the living room—center for a "game time," which occurred regularly in the afternoon on the long trips; some school lessons; discussions; and the like. The dining room changed from meal to meal—since it was the restaurant 200 miles away from the last meal. My games and toys were next to the back window.

In the front was an altimeter, which we always watched with interest when traveling through the Rockies or Sierras. The radio entertained us, though we didn't use it as frequently as it is often misused now.

There's no way around it—traveling 600 miles a day can get boring! Dad discovered many ways to keep himself occupied. He liked to sing. Those who have heard him attempt this feat in Sunday school, or start a hymn when the song leader was absent, will know why we did not encourage this habit. As in so many areas, it was next to impossible to control him. "Dad, that's enough!" I would say, more often than I can remember, and he would stop for a while. But I knew that the song was continuing in his mind, and that before long he would forget and burst out in whatever part of the verse he was in. An irrepressible desire to sing was basic to his character, I think. And though he had a keen mind, he often would be singing the simplest choruses—"Oh, happy day! Oh, happy day!" "I am Jesus' little man, / Yes, oh yes, oh yes, I am!"

If anyone practiced what he preached, it was Father. And he often preached that "good religion and good fun go hand in hand." Well, how do you have good fun in a car all day? We managed. We must have known about every automobile diversion there was: 20 Questions; going through the alphabet with billboard signs and license plates; games of Rook (always fun even if not always safe when the driver is trying to play too!); estimations about the mileage to the next desert horizon, where the road— a straight, thin thread—would finally disappear; reading or being read to. The latter took on more importance as I got older. In one trip across country, we might go through an entire long book, sometimes finishing up by flashlight. So often Dad would say, *"That* would make a good illustration!" or, "Boy, there's a thought"; and I wasn't at all surprised when the author or the passage turned up in

51

some sermon in the next meeting. As I got older, I might make it a special point to read a book I knew he wouldn't agree with; and often I would hear his side of the debate at the time, or later in another sermon.

The car, with its little areas set aside for play, sleep, discussion, prayer, was the unchanging house of that period. It changed only once every one or two years, when it was time to get another car. Nevertheless, this was our material "home," with its familiar objects. All else—everything around us—changed.

Then there was car trouble. Oh, those cars! We are always being reminded (for good reason) that the flesh is weak. But machines are weak too. One time it would be the generator; another, the regulator; the valves; the bearings; even the whole transmission. Sometimes professional opinion was divided as to just *what* the problem was. Dad traveled, in 10 years, close to 1 million miles, or twice to the moon and back; so the machines were bound to give out. And they weren't too particular just where.

Had it not been for the sudden decision of our car to go on strike, there are towns in the U.S. and Canada I would never have got to know so well: Amboy, Calif., in the middle of the Mojave Desert in summertime, for instance; other little towns in every state, where we would hopefully be spending a few hours and end up spending several days, while the mechanics found one problem after another; or the prairie country of Saskatchewan in the middle of a winter night, at 40° below—this time the car disabled by a flat tire (Dad, of course, had forgotten to bring along the proper gloves, and he ran back and forth from the rear tire to the front heater to warm up his hands); and the prairie country outside of Calgary, Alberta, also in the middle of the night, when Dad decided the problem lay in the spark plugs, pulled them all out, and discovered there are more ways of putting spark plug wires back than he had realized!

Considering the amount of car travel, we were very fortunate not to have more or worse accidents than we did. In all those years there were only a handful. Once, when Dad was pastor in Porterville, Calif., we were on a trip north. Near the Mount Shasta area, we drove over a hill only to discover the entire road was covered with ice on the north side. The car went out of control, turned completely over, back onto its wheels, and we went on. I remember (I was about eight) waking up under a pile of clothes to the sound of loud scraping. The top of the car was pushed in and badly dented in places. For a while after that, as Dad drove around Porterville, we put a sign on the car: "I Turned Over, You Turn Up at the Church of the Nazarene."

The whole experience of travel by car, especially in the 50s when roads were narrower and not always in the best condition, took on the qualities of adventure, complete with dangers. When Dad would ask the congregation, at the end of the revival meeting, to remember us in prayer; and when he preached, as he often did, on "How Far Are We Away from Home?" the last Sunday of the meeting, there was more in this than just convention or rhetoric. Travel was, and is, dangerous.

And a word about our weather at this point. I was abroad for two years; and, to my mind, nothing in the old country can compare with the blizzards of the prairies, the midwestern tornado, the desert flash flood, hailstorms, and hurricanes. Dad was in all of them. There were the times we would be driving in blinding rain, windshield wipers useless, with the radio on, listening for the location of tornado funnels. Through the all-but-deafening static from the lightning bolts, the announcer would say, "If you are travelling on Highway _____, there is one twister on your right, and another descending on your left. Be careful." The underpasses would be filled to capacity with cars and trailers, no room at all to take refuge. Hail has pounded the car, leaving dents all over it. My mother once found herself in the middle of a flash flood, with muddy water mixed with boulders roaring by.

Sometimes we would awake, breathing with difficulty, to find the motel filled with dust, knowing we had to start driving in an hour. We would start out with about one-foot visibility, usually following a truck, assuming, for some reason, that he could see better than we. Then there were the "black ice" conditions, the "silver freezes" in which cars were strewn all along the side of the road. No, when Dad asked the audience to pray for us in our travels, he wasn't just saying, "Have a nice week." He meant it and added to their prayers his own!

It is probably hard for anyone who hasn't lived this sort of life to understand or imagine it. Concert pianists, statesmen, entertainers, and evangelists know it well, though few are as completely free of a permanent residence as we were. In our case, it was one hotel, motel, guest house, or room after another, with restaurant food 90 percent of the time. And, most significant of all were the new faces every week—completely new faces! In the 50s, when Dad was doing the second period of his evangelism, the two-week, or one-and-a-half-week, meeting was more common than later. But still, there was just time to get to know some of the people, and then it was off to another city, usually another state.

Dad had a character unusually suited for this sort of life. It was a kind of restless spirit. He liked to be on the move. He liked the problems and challenges of his work to change frequently, take new forms. I haven't met many people who were as open to new experiences as he was.

His mind was a storehouse of them. One of the things that gave his ministry such a vitality was the virtually inexhaustible number of illustrations drawn from the people he had met: the scores that were saved, lives that ended in victory or tragedy, the little quirks of human character.

What developed through this constant changing of scene and constant exposure to new people was an ability to get along with, to relate to (in the terms of a later period), a great variety of personalities. "I am made all things to all men, that I might by all means save some" (1 Cor. 9:22), said by another Paul, who was also a traveler, applied very much to Paul Martin. This understanding of the variety in human character, and the fact, hard to accept by almost everyone, that there are people in the world who see things quite differently from you and with just as good a reason, was latent in his character always. But the years of travel increased and enriched this understanding immeasurably.

Still, everyone desires some kind of permanence. When arriving at the hotel we were to be in for a week, Dad wanted to take everything out of the car, including the chains. This was to be home—for a week. And so it was. The night we arrived, in would go all the luggage— every Samsonite case, the portable television set, racks of clothes, overnight bags, toys, boxes of books, music, records, phonograph, maps, shortwave radio (if detachable), golf clubs, tools, and much more. We would set up house as best we could.

In perhaps half of the meetings in the 50s, the evangelist and his family stayed in the pastor's home, the home of a prominent member, or an extra apartment attached to or below the church. This custom had obvious disadvantages and some positive aspects. Disadvantages included the lack of privacy, the exposure to domestic problems, the simple necessity of adjusting to someone else's schedule.

The positive aspects were harder to pin down and came into our awareness often long after the actual time. Nevertheless they were real. There was the opportunity to get to know a family very well; and to the extent that they reflected the nature of the church and the larger community, this knowledge was very helpful then and created exceedingly interesting memories later. In my mind, and I think in Dad's, the slight irritations and inconveniences of the week dissolved with time, and what was left was a colorful array of characters, comic and serious, unhappy to cheerful, absurd to inspired. And, in retrospect, a great richness was added to those years, making them seem fuller and longer than the more pleasing, more streamlined travel from motel to motel.

It was always with some worry that we approached the next meeting where we were due to stay at the parsonage or someone's home. We never knew what to expect. And our expectations were always wrong in some way or another. Once we arrived at a parsonage, our home for the next week, got out, and noticed that the sidewalks were iced over. Suddenly there came a booming voice: "Welcome to Slide Inn!" We knew what we were in for, and the jokes never let up through the week. We stayed upstairs and we knew when the meals were ready, for the same booming voice would announce, "Come and get it!" The pastor's wife, somewhat hypochondriac, was in bed with a mild cold all week long. But Dad made the most of the situation; on Sunday morning he arranged to have a bouquet of flowers at the front of the church, with a microphone hidden inside of it. He had all the members file around the bouquet and wish the pastor's wife a speedy recovery.

We stayed in one home where the wife continued to

56

bring up the deeds of the last evangelist—what he had done that was extraordinary. But they funneled into one main act, which she stated repeatedly: "He certainly made good ice cream!" Dad knew what was expected of him and held out for quite a while. But finally he gave in and offered to make it; and by Saturday afternoon, looking rather chagrined, he was cranking out ice cream for hours. What he didn't know was that she was taking it all inside to store in the freezer. He was actually the family ice cream maker for several months!

Sometimes we were given the children's room of the family, and it took the child quite a while to accept our occupation of his room. Sometimes he never did accept it and would come in at various times. On one occasion a piano was in that room, and the child would come in to practice, regardless of our situation at that moment. And we quickly learned that though the parents might reprove their children, under no circumstances should you attempt to do so.

On the other hand, there were times like our stay with Mrs. Emma Irick, then pastor at the Lufkin church in east Texas. In all our travels we never met a more enjoyable and inspirational Christian than she was. From the thoughtfulness in her hospitality (she would fix Dad and Mother coffee with cream and sugar every morning, and set it outside their door) to her absolute dedication to the church, its congregation, and the vast number of unsaved around the community, she represented to us an ideal model of what the pastor should be like. Her lunch and dinner conversation was witty and engaging, filled with fascinating stories of the holiness movement over the years (she had been at Pilot Point, Tex., at the historic founding). But above all there was the radiance of the Spirit-filled life. Yes, in meetings like that we left feeling more rewarded than when we came, glad of the opportunity to be in a radiant Christian's home.

The summer camps and camp meetings also had a different quality about them in those days. In the 50s they were far more a "camping out" experience. The suburbs had not spread out so far, and one felt fairly isolated just 10 or 20 miles out of town. And conditions were more "rustic"—to use a word that sounds more glamorous than the reality often was.

In certain parts of the country I had the definite feeling, when we started moving into our room at the camp, that we were greatly disturbing the nonhuman inhabitants, and that they would be far less willing to vacate for the week than the human families we usurped. Often my suspicions were correct, as the first evening would prove. An infinite variety of bugs would make an appearance then: grasshoppers, crickets, occasionally scorpions, tarantulas, spiders of all sorts. Sometimes they won the battle early, and we moved out to a motel before the week was over. In certain areas, snakes and centipedes roamed through and around the camp, providing a more persuasive deterrent to "absences without leave" than the strongest lectures on the part of the workers and ministers.

Sometimes the general camp conditions were less than ideal. There was the water, which had the color of tea from the rusty pipes. The rooms had a pungent smell of decayed wood. The screens over the windows had almost dissolved from rust. The weather sometimes affected the musical instruments during the months of disuse. I remember arriving at a camp that had just opened up. I played the piano and tried to practice every day. One time, when we arrived at a new place, I sat down at the instrument in the open-air auditorium of the camp and started a Chopin etude that begins at the top of the keyboard and descends to the middle, striking every note. It sounded beautiful. But the passage turns and ascends;

58

and as I began this part, not a note sounded. Every key I had depressed going down had stayed down! Light bulbs and even hair dryers were sometimes used to dry out the wood to keep the keys from sticking.

But the isolation and the semiprimitive conditions gave one the feeling of a genuine retreat, of living in another world for a week or two, where new friends were made, experiences were shared, love blossomed, minor hardships were overcome, and hopefully a better relationship with God was reached. Camp experiences are among my most vivid memories, and I am sure I am not alone in this. It seemed that the more they were different from the comfortable life back home, the greater the impression they made.

Dad fit into the camp and institute situation almost perfectly. For one thing, he always loved the outdoors—loved to "rough it." It might be inconvenient when he had to preach every night and morning, but he was used to that kind of life. His homes as a child had at times bordered on the primitive. And he loved nature, loved to get up in the morning and take a walk into the woods or the desert or the prairie, wherever the camp was. He loved the clean air of the country. And he liked the sports. He never, to the end of his life, felt obligated or forced to participate in the "Workers Versus the Teenagers" or the "Otters Versus the Raccoons" games—rather, he played in these as often as he could. We would more often have to caution him about overexerting and try to cool the enthusiasm a bit.

Getting to know the teenagers at this level always increased his ability later in the day at services and campfires to talk seriously to them, to preach to them, to exhort them to strive for a better Christian life. It was the whole experience, from the fun times to the serious, that he enjoyed. Every institute or camp meeting week was a little

59

like a "Life in a Nazarene Parsonage" all over, with its days of fun, days of humorous embarrassment, and days of victory.

During the week, Dad's belief in wholesome family activity, in the joys of adventure, found greater play. Some of the fondest memories I will ever have are of the day trips we took during the revival meeting week, the places we explored—from the automobile factories of Detroit, to the U.S. Mint in Washington, D.C., to the little roads that lead nowhere in particular for 30 miles, visiting a church member's beehive, national parks and monuments, collecting maple tree sap, or hiking up the hill behind the motel. In the Midwest, during tornado warnings, you might not find us at the motel or in a shelter. More likely you would find us out driving, looking at the clouds and the lightning!

Of the many memories of the days of fun in our traveling parsonage, I will mention, in closing, only a few. Dad liked to fish. His father, part Indian, was an excellent fisherman, catching fish at times with only his hands. Dad would take me on day fishing trips, particularly in the northwest part of the country, where were the rivers and streams he knew the best. He had his own style. Never have I heard of anyone else who fished in a business suit! But that's the way he did it—even if he had to climb 5 to 10 miles from the road through thick undergrowth. I can see him now, standing knee-deep in the middle of the stream, dressed in last year's preaching outfit, pulling in fish after fish, putting them in his pocket if the other containers were full.

He liked to hike. We went on hikes in every meeting, if there were any areas to hike in. Once, when I first saw Yosemite Valley, I was naturally anxious to take to the trails. I had arrived with another family the day before and had no doubt been badgering them to take a hike

On Half Dome in Yosemite (c. 1959)

with me (I was 11 and eager to take the most challenging
trail). Finally the man gave in, and we started toward
Vernal Falls.

Vernal Falls in the spring is a torrent of water, and
the boulders at the bottom send mist up the nearby trail
in torrents. This spring was particularly wet (it was the
year of the Yuba City floods), and it was soon apparent
that we would get soaked. At the first sign of mist, the
man I was with suggested we go back. I didn't protest.
I knew who would be arriving later that day. And I knew
that, mist or no mist, he would want to get to the top of

61

the falls. Later that afternoon, two people, one young and the other middle-aged, hiked up the trail again, getting thoroughly soaked and thoroughly happy.

Dad kept his interest in hiking throughout his life. Even when he began to get pains which were later diagnosed as angina pains, it was still hard to keep him off the trail. After his first heart attack, he was still convinced that he might be able to climb into the high Sierras, given enough time and preparation. Fortunately, his busy schedule prevented his attempting this.

There is a rock in Yosemite, on the way to Yosemite Falls, called "prayer rock." No one knows it by this name except three people: Paul Skiles, Dad, and me. One morning, Dad and I started up the trail very early, about 4 a.m. The trail ascends "as if on wings," John Muir wrote. At a certain point, the great silhouette of Half Dome came into view. The sight was so astonishing and beautiful that Dad said, "Why don't we have a prayer, here at this rock." It was a medium-size boulder at the end of one of the switchbacks. We did and went on to the top. Every time we went up there after that, we would have a prayer at that spot; and when Paul Skiles, then a music-evangelist and youth worker on the Northern California District, hiked that trail with us later, we had a prayer there, too.

Seventeen years later I was on that trail once again. The world had changed so much, and so had all of us. Dad was no longer able to hike that kind of trail. I was hiking alone. I wasn't sure I would find the rock; there are so many medium-size boulders in that area. But sure enough, at the end of one of the switchbacks, the sight of Half Dome once again appeared, and there to the right was the same flattened rock. I paused for a prayer there, filled with the memories of those days of fun that Dad and I had.

8

The Chinese Church

By the time Michael reached high school age, it was clear that a new solution would have to be sought to the "family vs. travel" problem. Paul and Monica could no longer remain teachers. And yet for them to travel while Michael stayed with other members of the family seemed unsatisfactory. The solution came with a suggestion from Dr. George Coulter, then district superintendent of the Northern California District. His idea was that Paul pastor the Chinese Church of the Nazarene in San Francisco on a part-time basis, the other time being used to continue his evangelistic work.

His decision to accept this position startled some of his friends. Why would such a well-known evangelist, whose successes and popularity were increasing with each year, deliberately choose a small home mission church and run the risk of being all but forgotten by the larger community of Nazarenes? Why, if he did want to pastor, did he not accept a larger, more prestigious church?

There were several reasons. The one, already mentioned, deserves to be mentioned again. His sermons on the home and the importance of the family as a center for fun and spiritual growth were not ideas that were dropped after leaving the pulpit. He believed in them passionately. They were at the source of his own upbringing. The idea of being a father and husband in absentia was something he could not accept. This particular position offered the best situation, for he could also evangelize. As to the size of the church, Paul was quite unambitious in this respect. It mattered more to him that he had some time to travel, that he could be near his family, and that he was in a community he enjoyed, felt at home in. As for the latter, San Francisco and the Chinese community proved ideal.

Paul and Monica had fallen in love with San Francisco from the first time they were in the city, during their first evangelistic period. Monica's uncle, Donnell Smith, had pastored the first church there. During their travels in the 50s they began to think of San Francisco more and more as a "second home." If enough meetings were close by, they would stay in a reasonable hotel there for a month at a time. It seemed natural to settle down in this city, when the time came.

The Chinese community, with its exciting, varied culture and the dedicated members that made up the church, would make fascinating material for any number of books. There are few communities anywhere that can rival the vitality and diversity of this, the largest Oriental center outside of the Orient itself. Anyone who has visited this part of San Francisco is aware of this aspect, and the complexity and fascination increase the more one stays there.

Paul, Monica, and Michael grew to love Chinese food—and Paul and Michael acquired an acceptable proficiency with chopsticks. They went to the elaborate banquets, which occupy a vital place in the social life of the community and which feature the rarer delicacies such as bird's nest soup or shark's fin soup, along with the ever-popular "four-star cider," which is a combination of apple juice and soda water. They visited families during the Chinese New Year in February and went to the big parades, with their dragons, floats, exotic musical instruments, and continuous explosions of fireworks. Pastoral calls were now to places like the Cathay Bazaar, where Mrs. Bock worked as manager; a sewing machine factory, where some of the ladies worked; or a kitchen of one of the large Grant Avenue restaurants, where some of the men cooked. He got to know prominent people in the family associations, like Mr. Chin, who was also one of the main members of the church.

The Chinese church and parsonage are still in one building. The church is on the ground floor, in what was once a garage. The second floor, during the days of Paul's ministry there, was used as a Chinese school during the week, where Chinese children were taught written Chinese. On Sundays, this second floor was given over to Sunday school classes. The third floor is the parsonage. The fourth floor consists of one room, a penthouse, which Michael had as his room. The views, especially from the penthouse, are magnificent, with an excellent view of Coit Tower across the valley of North Beach through one window, Alcatraz through another, and Russian Hill through a third. Paul, when he grew nervous or tense about the demands and challenges of this pastorate, would look across to Alcatraz Island from the kitchen, where he often worked, and think: "No matter how bad it is here, it's worse over there!"

This period was a time of challenge for both pastor and congregation! Most of the other ministers at the church had been Chinese, so there had been no problem with interpretation/translation. Paul, however, had to speak through an interpreter every Sunday morning. The evening service and prayer meeting were usually attended by people with enough command of English to get along without translation. Imagine Paul Martin, known for his rapid-fire delivery, his almost breathless excitement, when the words seemed to pour in a continuous stream, having to stop after every other sentence while the thought was conveyed in Chinese! And there were other problems to overcome. Jokes in English, relying on idiomatic expressions, would be incomprehensible in Chinese unless the interpreter stopped to explain the original meaning; and by then the joke would be hardly worth the trouble. Certain expressions that have a tremendous emotional impact in English may mean next to nothing in Chinese, and vice versa.

I have always thought that this obstacle to be overcome was a great blessing in disguise. It imposed on Dad a kind of discipline that made his preaching even more effective as time went on, and not just to the Chinese congregation but to all audiences. He had to slow down, consider how best and most concisely to express an idea, to clarify his thinking and speaking. I began to notice among other audiences that he was growing more careful in how he expressed things, thereby strengthening the power of his message greatly. He found he didn't have to act excited and hilarious all the time to get across an idea effectively.

And he began to find ways to explain spiritual truths over the barriers of language and culture. This talent was an extension of the ability he had already acquired to communicate to varieties of people throughout the United States. But the challenge was even greater at the Chinese Church. And it was an ability he was later to use effectively in his travels to South America and to Europe.

I remember an older Chinese lady who knew almost no English. Some of us Caucasians had great difficulty communicating with her, and often our attempts at conversations dwindled to embarrassing silences, while both would wait for someone else to arrive. When Paul met this lady, he plunged into conversation in simple English, and she immediately responded in simple Chinese; and before long they were laughing, gesturing, having a grand time, each hardly understanding a word the other was saying! But somehow, in spite of it all, they were getting the basic ideas across.

It was a challenging time for the congregation as well. Getting used to a Caucasian evangelist who didn't know a word of Chinese and was gone half the time took some doing. Frank Jow, a member of the church at that time, and a good friend of the Martin family, recalls: "One incident seemed to show the stress and strain in the life of an evangelist-pastor, the rush and hurry type of pace that was intensified by making plane schedules and revival meetings around the country and the world. One Saturday, after taking the Sunday school boys to play baseball, I instructed them to do something nice for Rev. Martin—to wash his car and to bake him a pizza from one of those supermarket pizza kits. Well, the kids were in the process of drying the car when Rev. Martin came through like a tornado, took the car and left hurriedly, with water droplets still unwiped on the car, the boys with their mouths wide open and rags in their hands, and the pizza untouched. Such was a man who, during his earthly life, deeply loved the Lord, cared for souls, and went about his Father's business seriously."

One lady, in the Wednesday night prayer meeting, during the part of the month that Paul was away, prayed (and this prayer was said often and without sarcasm), "Bless Brother Martin, wherever he is!"

Nevertheless, pastor and congregation grew to understand and enjoy each other and to develop spiritually.

Years later, at Dad's funeral, there were many familiar faces I had not seen for years. I realized more at that time the effect his ministry had had on that congregation. Ruby Fong, one of the fine Christians of the Chinese Church at that time, says: "I remember Paul Martin as a concerned man. He knew you as a person. He remembered your hurts, your feelings, your joys and sorrows. He was there when I needed him and God. When Paul Martin prayed, I could feel God's presence. He went right to the point of need, and God heard and answered."

Stanley Louie, who was the young people's president then and is now a member of the Santa Ana church, says:

> It was about Christmastime in 1957 when Rev. Paul Martin came to pastor the Chinese Church in San Francisco. Our church was a young mission church. Many of us were newly converted Christians. My wife and I were among them. During those years, Rev. Martin took a personal interest in every one of us. He was fun to be with. His love and caring continued to influence the lives of my wife and myself. I remember on one of his visits to our home, we shared with him some of the obstacles of becoming a Christian because of our cultural background. He was very understanding, and he taught us to be patient and tactful to our loved ones who had not yet believed in Jesus Christ; but that we should always be ready to take stands for our belief. Our desires to serve the Lord grew stronger day by day as we shared fellowship with Rev. Martin through the years as our pastor.
>
> We moved to southern California in 1962. It was about the same time Rev. Martin left the Chinese Church to become a full-time evangelist. His personal interest in us continued. We remained in good contact. He helped us to find a wonderful church in Santa Ana where my family are now deeply committed to serving the Lord. Every time he came to preach at churches around the area, he always found time to visit us. Each time we enjoyed our fellowship tremendously. His ministry meant a great deal to me and my family.

In 1961, Michael was in college at the University of California, Berkeley, and Paul decided it was time to return to the world of full-time evangelism. The family moved across town to a little apartment in the Sunset District of San Francisco, which was to be a sort of home, a place to come back to, in between tours. Michael lived there and commuted to Berkeley, and Monica's mother, who had been taking vacations with the family, settled permanently with the Martin family at their home in San Francisco.

From that time on the family was always to keep an apartment in the Bay Area: San Francisco, Berkeley, or Oakland. Certain times could be counted on for bringing us together—one or two days before Christmas, especially—but from now on Paul's work was to be continuously on the road.

9

Paul Martin—Humorist, Exhorter, Revivalist

From 1962 to the end of his life, Paul was to remain a full-time evangelist. Occasionally he would think of settling down again, but never very seriously. He knew that he was now doing his lifework. It is interesting to note that each time he reentered the field of full-time evangelism, he received a call to a large church and therefore had to think through his decision carefully. It seemed that his dedication to this particular calling was being tested each time.

These last 15 years were a culmination of his work, a period of increasing success and popularity, a fulfillment of his calling to preach the gospel to all the world. What were the reasons for this unusually effective ministry? What was there about him and his message that allowed him to be such a capable tool in the spreading of the gospel? I can think of three areas in which he excelled: humor, exhortation, and his treatment of the revival week in all its aspects.

It is hard to write about someone's humor—certainly better to quote him! Extensive analysis seems more out of place here than in most areas. But a few observations may be appropriate. I don't think it is unobjective for me to say that he was one of the funniest preachers the church has ever known. His sense of timing, his ability to catch you off guard, his awareness of the amusing sides to almost any situation are recognized and have been described often. His jokes and ironic twists while speaking were so natural because they were "him" throughout his life—in his letters, books, conversations with friends and relatives, his dealings with everyone from bank clerks to executives, waiters, and fellow preachers. To spend much time with him was to experience the joyous, healing effects of laughter. And it was contagious. I and many others began to liven up, to see the humor in otherwise gloomy things, to joke about the world when it needed joking about.

He never felt entirely comfortable with an audience unless they could laugh with him. Similar to his feeling that "if you can play with a boy, you might be able to pray with him," was the conviction that if you can share fun and laughter with an audience, you might be able to talk seriously with them later. So he would often start his sermon in that lighthearted spirit for which he was so well known. And, by extension, the first service of his revival week would often be on the humorous, lighter side.

If necessary, he would sometimes go to extreme lengths to get the audience in a happy, humorous mood. Dr. Uerkvitz, who was with Father on the South American tour, recalls that in Barbados, Father was to speak to a group of boys who had had to stay after school to hear him. They weren't all that pleased to be there and were very resistant to his jokes and funny anecdotes. He tried them all with no success. Finally he resorted to the simplest, most basic form of humor—the funny face. A series of funny faces—that finally cracked the ice! Before long they were listening to him as well as watching him.

There was an important quality to this humor. Dr. Zachary expressed it well when he said, "He loved banter, but I never heard him say a malicious word to, or about, anybody." In this sense, he was the exact opposite of the scathing satirist, the unkind mimic, or the person who elicits laughter at the expense of a culture or a race. Anyone he made jokes about, and I was one of them, felt equally at home in the service, hearing them, as he did if he were absent. It was a humor that, for all its bite and perception, was curiously gentle.

And he always included himself. If people were funny, then no one was funnier than the fellow on the platform! I can't resist one example: in the "Life Story" sermon, he describes the time his older brother Ted ran away from home. He always enjoyed ribbing Ted; the lifelong banter between these two brothers was a recurrent theme over the decades. In this instance, he describes the note left behind, the halfhearted attempt to leave the town, the night in the hay across from the mental institution, when every driver who passed by was afraid to pick him up!

But those who remember this illustration knew about the other amusing character in it—the brother who was just as happy that his older brother was gone, who would get more peace at nighttime, who couldn't quite share in the rest of the family's concern—in other words, Paul himself. The poignant climax comes when Ted, returning home, looking through the kitchen window, expecting to find a family indifferent to his decision, finds "five saints *and one other*" on their knees in prayer! This is a perfect example of self-inclusion in this serious-comic situation. Often Paul opened his humorous sermons with some jokes about himself.

Another characteristic of his humor—quite an original characteristic, I always thought—was how quickly it might change into the serious. The opening of his life

72

story is again illustrative. Often audiences found themselves still laughing when he was already deadly serious. There was at times a jumble of reactions in the audience as they attempted to change gears. It was a highly unconventional, yet effective kind of rhetoric. And it was more. It reflected very well that odd mixture of comedy and seriousness which characterizes so many of the incidences of our lives. It caught the complexity of the humorous response—the sudden perception of the serious even while one is laughing.

Humor is always about something. If one has the inclination to analyze it, he will discover the often disguised, complex message. For Paul, the preacher, there was always a basically simple, overriding aim: how to better communicate the gospel message, how to better win souls for Christ. And it was an example in itself of his often said remark that "there are more things that are fun and right than fun and wrong."

If humor was an effective tool, so was his ability to exhort. Ted recalls:

> Very early in our relationship as fellow camp meeting preachers, I saw that Paul had a unique gift. I like to think of it as the gift of exhortation. I think our mother had such a gift as well. Often, as Paul has told, she could take over in a service, when Dad was preaching, with a shouting spell to be followed by a warmhearted exhortation. By the time she was through, Dad was ready to go on with renewed fervor. So it was with Paul. Not that he interrupted anyone but himself.
>
> One incident I shared in made an indelible mark on my memory and heart. We were fellow preachers at a camp meeting. It was Paul's turn to preach, and there was a large and expectant crowd who listened intently. But Paul was having one of his rare, difficult times moving into the emotional rhythm so characteristic of his ministry. I don't think he had been

speaking more than 10 minutes when he suddenly stopped.

"Now I can preach better than this," he said to the surprised audience. "And you know it! But what I'm trying to do is to get you to move close to God. Will everyone stand?" He then proceeded to give a 10- to 15-minute warmhearted exhortation for people who needed to settle issues between themselves and God, asking them to come forward to the altar of prayer and to do so at once. It was the kind of earnest plea that people around the world have heard and responded to, often weeping openly. The singing of an invitation song was not needed, for a steady stream of people in every aisle of that tabernacle moved to the altar. It and the front were filled, and prayer warriors hurried to join them. Prayer rose from voices everywhere throughout the building, and camp meeting was on!

Several abilities were the basis of this exhortative power. One was the courage to be spontaneous—risking, on the one hand, possible misunderstanding or confusion on the part of the audience; on the other hand, attaining those brilliant flashes that only unpremeditated wit and perception can have. However, like other successful practitioners of the art of improvisation, he knew the value of careful, ordered preparation—realizing that the clearly ordered sermon is a necessary framework to inspired departures. So, as Ted said, he "interrupted himself"; though, like his father, he was ready to go point by point through the prepared sermon from start to finish. Like his mother, he was ready to have a verbal "shouting spell," an outburst of humor, a sudden insight, when the Spirit led. And the prepared sermon was always there for his return when he might conclude his excursion with, "And may God add His blessing to that thought."

Always the audience was uppermost in his mind. Was he getting through to them? If not, he was willing to do anything to get back and hold their interest. He realized always that if the audience is not with you, the most beautifully organized and intelligent sermon in the world is merely a series of words. I've seen him change sermons halfway through; or suddenly stop, as Ted writes, and begin an exhortation; or even start the same sermon three times, complete with the same introductory remarks: "Is that clear? Are you following me? No, I don't think so. O.K., let's start again. Say, it's wonderful to be here this evening! . . ."

In a sense, he was always wary of "preaching for its own sake." He was skillful enough with words to know how easily they can be misused or become an end in themselves. He often referred to Paul's remark about the "foolishness of preaching" (1 Cor. 1:21), expanding the application to include, beside the unsaved, unresponsive listener, the intentions of the speaker himself. This was one reason why he would depart from the ordered sermon and attempt to get to that particular audience at that particular time. And it was why he was never satisfied to be only a platform figure, why his revivals included so much calling and other person-to-person contact.

He also knew the limitations of the single service. To influence, to guide, to communicate may take longer than just one evening, no matter how good or inspired you are. This leads me to the third area in which Paul excelled: how he handled the revival week.

But first, it might be appropriate to briefly describe the daily schedule he followed during the week, since this relates to the actual results of the revival meeting. In these years, he lived more by a schedule than might have been apparent. Some kind of routine is always necessary to conserve energy, and this was especially the case with Paul, who was on the go all the time.

He was an early riser by this time in his life—always up by 5:30 or 6:00 at the latest. He would write for an hour and a half before breakfast, the time when he felt mentally clearest. Often breakfast would be spent with one of the men in the church—someone who needed help or that Paul could be of value to—or with the pastor. Then it was back to his room for more writing. He spent about three hours each day working on these writing projects: articles for the *Herald* or *Come Ye Apart,* devotionals, and books.

Lunch would often be another church-related time: either a women's luncheon or lunch with another member. He invariably rested an hour in the afternoon; it really hurt his day if he didn't get in this afternoon sleep. Then there was answering letters, responding to revival meeting calls, working out the complicated dates (he was always booked two to three years in advance). He and Monica always tried to keep dinner for themselves—a rest from all the social obligations. Then he spent an hour cleaning and freshening up. This was quite important to him— increasingly so as time went on. He didn't want anything to detract from the evening message such as a sloppy or unkempt appearance.

Then he would prepare for the evening service, ordering things well so that he could preach according to plan, or change, if the Spirit led. After the main evening service, there was usually another get-together for the teenagers, young adults, young marrieds, and, more recently, singles, which would really develop into a mini-service, with Paul preaching about 10 minutes more. Then it was home and to bed quite soon.

The revival week itself developed into a definite pattern, the product of his years of experience before a wide variety of audiences. He might change this pattern, and often did so, if the occasion warranted it; still, it remained as a kind of structure, an order to the variations. There were two crucial points he always kept in mind in this pattern: (1) the importance of the sequence of sermons, how they should be placed in the week; and (2) the importance of establishing a more personal connection with his audience than just via the platform.

The usual week was Tuesday over Sunday, with Monday spent in travel. Tuesday night was the introductory night, and he often introduced a scripture that would become a motto for the week. His favorite text for this was Ps. 84:11, "For the Lord God is a sun and shield: the Lord will give grace and glory: no good thing will he withhold from them that walk uprightly." No good thing! Was there a good thing that could happen during the week—an answer to prayer? Was there someone who needed to be saved or sanctified? A problem that needed working out? He usually had the audience repeat this text every night of the revival and would ask for raised hands if a "good thing" had happened already. It became the overriding theme of the week. Once, while holding a meeting at the College Church at Olivet, he received a 3 a.m. phone call by students in one of the dorms. "Brother Martin, say, with me, Ps. 84:11: 'For . . .'" He was too sleepy to come up with any humorous response—not until later in the week! But he knew what he was doing—knew that an overriding idea, a simple thing to look forward to, to strive for, was extremely important to hold the week together.

After the first service, he would often ask for the men of the church to meet him on the platform. He would arrange for one of them to act as leader in arranging a men's breakfast later in the week, inviting as many outsiders as possible as well as the regular members for this fellowship. Similarly, a delegate would be chosen to work out the plan for the women's luncheon.

During the middle of the week, Wednesday or Thursday, he would preach on love and forgiveness, and have a "love feast." The sermon would not be too long, and he

77

would relegate the last 10 minutes or so to this "feast." The congregation was asked to go and whisper to each other one of three things: (1) "I'm sorry, forgive me," if there was a misunderstanding or a grievance that needed righting; (2) "I appreciate you," if that needed to be said or reinforced; or (3) "I'm praying for you." No one else would know what was said. The altar was open for anyone who wished to pray, though no altar call was used. The organist would play such songs as "Blest Be the Tie That Binds" or "Oh, How I Love Jesus." Often many sought the Lord in this warm, yet informal, atmosphere.

On another evening he would often use a format his Brother Ted had also used—the E. Stanley Jones open altar service. No final exhortation or pleading. The lights would be darkened, the organist would play four verses of "Jesus, I Come," and anyone could come forward for any reason and stay as long as he wished. After the fourth verse, those who stayed would be prayed with, if they so wished. The format appealed to Paul because there was little emotional manipulation (which he was always suspicious of), little division between degrees of spiritual attainment, and no accumulation of seekers for the sake of it—just an openness, a receptivity to God.

Friday night was often the night for the "dark room" sermon. This had evolved over the years from an elaborate candlelight service in the earlier days. At one time, each member of the audience was given a good-sized candle. In the early days, each person, in fact, could go wherever he wanted to in the building or on the campgrounds to pray. The climax of the service was Paul's quoting the Lamplighter's poem, "I shall light my lamp from faith's white spark, / And through this wild storm hold it high!" "It makes a difference!" he would say, and indeed it would, as the whole auditorium brightened with this extra light.

In time, he stopped using the candles, what with great reservations on the part of the fire department, complaints from the janitors who had to remove the wax from the rugs, and even those who felt the audience might get hypnotized from staring at the flame! But the dark room part of the sermon remained—the "dark room" everyone must go through, of indecision, worry, or fear—just as Samuel experienced as he remained all night before the high priest's room.

Vital to the service was a time of silence—no music, no speaking, a darkened auditorium—to let the dark room of one's troubles settle in on him. Paul usually asked three people to come forward to pray during this time: a teenager who was an outstanding Christian and who commanded respect among his peers, and two prominent laymen. At the end of the silent period, which always seemed longer than it actually was, the organist would start playing, and Paul would remind us that "standing somewhere in the shadows, you'll find Jesus." Each of the three would be asked to stand and tell the congregation if God had laid a burden on their heart, and what it was. Not a testimony, but a burden for the church.

If it seemed the right thing to do, this part of the meeting would be followed by an old-fashioned altar service. Of course, nothing is, or should be, perfectly ordered. In this case, the great room for variation came in just what those people would say! Most of them conveyed a real burden that hit the spot in everyone's concerns for their church. Some wanted to testify. A few wanted to discuss their family problems or where they were going to move to. And I'll never forget one man who rose and said, "Well, Brother Martin, God hasn't told me a thing yet! But I'll keep praying!"

This sermon and its format had the important effect of making all participants more aware of the burdens they were carrying, their prayers for their church, the unsaved they knew and had been praying for—in other words, all the "good things" they still wanted done. After this weightier Friday evening service, he often would "let off steam" with the Saturday night service—at which he would give the always-asked-for "Life in a Nazarene Parsonage" or another humorous message. Throughout this time, the other, "unseen" side of the week's program had been going on: the men and women's prayer breakfasts and luncheons, the separate meals with important people, the calling with the pastor, the times with the teenagers and young adults.

Sunday morning was the climax of all this work. He would ask the pastor which Sunday school class would benefit the most from his speaking to them for 20 minutes or so—usually it was the teens or young marrieds. Often a number would feel the need for a stronger commitment from this Sunday school time.

In the morning service, he used an idea that came out of his "thoughtful moments" with musical accompaniment years ago. He would ask the organist to play a series of hymns—"Jesus Loves Me," "The Wedding March," "Abide with Me," and "The Old Rugged Cross"—while he spoke of the altar at the front of the church; its special place in everyone's hearts, where babies were dedicated, young people married, older people were laid to rest, and, greatest of all, where people came to make their commitment to God. If it seemed the right thing to do, he would have an altar service right at that point before speaking or even in lieu of it. (He always knew the value of not speaking as well as the value of speaking.) Here, too, the unpredictable sometimes arose, as when the pastor misunderstood the format and assumed that this musical presentation was the end of the service and dismissed the people!

After these moments, Paul would launch into a very serious sermon, such as "How Far Are You from Home?" Many people sought the Lord in these Sunday morning services, and there were many answers to prayer, many "good things" done at this time. Often, at the end of the service, he would have the congregation group itself into families, including his own, and have the pastor pray a general prayer for them and the church. This last idea—the "family service"—is remembered especially by the many who participated in it. He usually asked that one member of the family speak to the others about their spiritual needs—quietly, without embarrassment. To have the families together and in prayer was more than just a device. It was a summary of his deepest spiritual beliefs.

Many evangelists have a very weighty, strong final service on Sunday evening. Paul tended toward the opposite. It was usually his most optimistic sermon, often on the text "Behold, I have set before thee an open door, and no man can shut it" (Rev. 3:8). He would expound upon the future, the opportunities of the church in the days ahead.

Two reasons were behind this choice of ending message. One was Paul's deep-seated optimism, goodwill, and cheerfulness. He wanted, above all, for people to be left with a positive, uplifting spirit and motivation. The second was his realization that while he had commanded the attentions of the congregation for a week, the real future of the church and its development lay with the congregation and its pastor. In the message, he, in effect, returned the pastor to his rightful position and gave him his whole-hearted support. One might note, in this regard, that Paul did not like to stay very long after the last service. As soon as possible, he was back to the motel and usually packed up and was away that very night. His work was over; it was time for the church to push forward on its own.

I think it was this format, with its de-emphasis on altar services as a spectacle, heavy emotionalism, rigid revivalistic procedures, or "star-oriented" entertainments that allowed him to continue to work so successfully, at a time when the concept of revivalism was being called into question and the rhetorical devices of another era were declining. For, regardless of the time or the place, people still have the same basic needs: They still need revival in their hearts; they need those "good things," those answers to prayer; they need a God-centered family; and they need a strong, optimistic church. Someone who can be instrumental in satisfying those needs will always have a place.

10

"Every Evangelist Ought
to Have a Book..."

"Every evangelist ought to have a book, a record, cassette tapes, oil filters, vaporizers, cough medicine..." Paul would often begin, on his "book advertising" night. Well, he didn't sell all of that! But he did make a record of his sermon "Life in a Nazarene Parsonage." And, of course, he wrote many books that were sold during the meetings as well as nationwide in Nazarene and other Christian bookstores.

"Many speakers who sell books and records will tell you that they have only a few left, just a remainder from the big sales of the last meeting; so that if you want to buy them, you'd better hurry to the booth after the service. Not in our case. We have a whole trunk full of these things that we're dying to get rid of; you couldn't buy us out if you had to! Another thing you will hear is that all the money received from the books will go to foreign missions or to an important charity. Well, all the money Mrs. Martin and I receive from our books *goes right into our own pockets!*"

What made the last remarks so funny was their complete truth. The first book of "Life in a Nazarene Parsonage" was printed up at Paul and Monica's expense in Walla Walla, Wash. It was just the size of a pamphlet. But there were so many of them that they filled up the large trunk of the car completely. They were eager to sell them, not only for the small revenue they brought in, but for the extra packing space! Later, the publishing house told Father they would like to clear out their surplus of the "Life in a Nazarene Parsonage" record. The result again was a trunk filled with boxes of records. At such times it would have taken a large rally indeed to exhaust the supply!

The record of "Life in a Nazarene Parsonage" was brought out in 1963. Typical of Dad was the semiprimitive way it came in existence. In 1959, he and I went to two summer camps together, flying in the new 707 jets. We were 40 pounds overweight, due largely to my excessive luggage, which included much of my library, my slides, photography equipment, and tape recorder. This last item, a little Wollensak, proved the most useful. In the Upper New York camp, there were direct connections from the microphones to the outlets at the back of the auditorium, so I decided to tape several sermons, including "Life . . ." It lay around in the closet for a number of years, and it was brought out occasionally to play for relatives and friends. When the decision was made to publish a record, we remembered this tape. It is about as much the opposite of a studio job as it can be: limited fidelity, no rehearsal, no idea it would become a record at all. But the audience is live, and the message has a spontaneity it may have lost, had it been recorded under more professional circumstances.

Paul's interest in writing started early. From the time of his first pastorate and evangelistic work, he was trying his hand at articles, even poems, and publishing some of them. I recall seeing a piece of emblematic verse, a poem in the shape of a cross, which dated from his student years.

His first "book"—the first version of the life story mentioned above—was completed about the time he started evangelizing again after the Porterville pastorate. It sold for something like 10 cents. Later, he expanded the book considerably, when it was published by Beacon Hill Press. Actually, it was a collection of articles he had written for the *Herald of Holiness* on the "Life in a Nazarene Parsonage" theme. Already the anthology or collection of shorter articles to form a book was his preferred format, and he wrote in this style throughout his life. They suited his personality—these short, witty embellishments of an inspirational thought or event that had caught his attention or had taken place in his life. In a sense, his style was an extension of the way he wrote letters.

A word, at this point, about Paul Martin, the letter writer. I have already mentioned his habit of writing continuously to those in need of help, guidance, or consolation. But he wrote often when there was no special reason. In an age when fewer and fewer write letters, depending on the phone for important communication and waiting until paths cross to have discussion, Father was a definite exception. My grandmother, his mother-in-law, received three letters a week on the average, and I received about the same number. Mother got almost one a day. (This did not include postcards, pamphlets, newspapers from various towns, which were also sent in abundance.) His relatives and friends heard from him frequently.

I try to keep all the letters I receive, to read over and enjoy through the years. In the case of my dad's letters, this habit presented a special problem. After a year or two, an entire drawer would be filled with them, and they would have to be stored elsewhere to make room for the new ones! Sometimes he would enclose a stack of post-cards, often having written on the back of each one. No one wrote him as often as he wrote them, I think, nor did he expect it.

The letters were rarely long, at most two pages of moderately large script. There was little to no trace of the stilted quality that characterizes so many letters. The sheer volume of them ironed out that problem over the years. When we opened letters from him, it was like a brief conversation; we could hear him saying most everything he wrote. And every letter, no matter how short, had some little flash of humor, some unexpected perception or way of expressing something that made it really worthwhile.

From this correspondence, his family who was not traveling with him at the time knew not only where he had been every week, but the weather, kind of country it was, anecdotes about the people there, the most amusing thing that happened to him while there, occasional afterthoughts about politics and current events, and always a spiritual "thought for the day." He had a very unforced way of introducing the last mentioned, so that even his non-Christian relatives and friends were never alienated by these thoughts. It was the same unforced quality that made his devotionals so effective.

His second book was also a compilation of *Herald* articles about successful Nazarene laymen. It came out under the title *Ask the Man Who Has It—Stories of Real Men Who Found a Real Savior;* and it related the experiences of such men as Dr. Wilfong, who had already done important work with synthetic fabrics ("Dacron, Orlon, and Wilfong" was the title, I believe); Bud Smee, Roy Smee's son, then district attorney in California; Gordon Olson; the inventor of the Ford retractable hardtop; and many others.

As with his speaking, a natural talent was there, but

it was refined and improved by years of almost continuous practice. He contributed countless articles to the *Herald, Standard,* and *Discoveries* (formerly *Junior Joys*) throughout the years of evangelism and pastoring.

In 1962, at the beginning of his last and most extensive period of evangelism, he was asked to write a devotional for teens. It was the perfect assignment for him. He had the years of experience working and playing with teenagers behind him; he spoke their language. He had a wealth, an almost inexhaustible storehouse of experiences to draw upon, of people and places across the country; and he felt at home with the "devotional" length from his numerous articles. What developed more with this book was its informal, witty style—his way of presenting spiritual truths in a seemingly effortless manner, and the variety of presentations.

I remember well the time he was writing this first devotional book. It was in our apartment in San Francisco, just after he had left the Chinese Church. Every once in a while he would come into my room and say, "Mike, how does this sound?" or "Am I crazy, or is this a good way of putting this idea?" Already I was struck by the greater novelty of expression. And he seemed to be especially involved in this writing. As it turned out, this book, which was finally called *Good Morning, Lord,* was his most successful one up to that time—the one which really made him known as an inspirational writer of real humor and originality. The book was launched at the second International Institute, in Estes Park, Colo., and its success spread throughout the country. It settled Paul into his style of writing books from that time on.

The titles of the subsequent devotionals reveal, as Dr. E. E. Zachary said, "a zest and joy of living"—*Get Up and Go! Have a Good Day! Good Night, Lord;* and *Family Fare.* But like his sermons, there was a strong element of the serious. Side by side with the sporting anecdotes, the rules and advice on rock-throwing contests, were the descriptions of tragedies he had witnessed, thoughts on death and the impermanency of this world. This counterplay was a trademark of both his speaking and writing. And one of the most appealing things about the devotionals, I think, was the fact that one could "hear" him while reading—his speaking and writing style were very close. One was not struck by a sudden stiffness when meeting the person on the written page.

There were a few projects that were never completed that reflect a more serious vein. He did a good deal of work on a book about the last sayings of people well known worldwide or just within the church. Although he never published this work, it provided a good many illustrations for material in sermons. But it was the combination of the humorous and the serious, the blending of one imperceptibly into the other that was his most engaging style and that most reflected his own personality.

11

"... and One Other"

Several chapters ago, there was included Paul's description of Ted's attempt to run away from home, his night in the hay, and his return to find "five saints and one other" around the kitchen table in prayer. In a sense, the phrase "and one other" could be used to describe a side of Paul people knew and loved throughout his life: not the "otherness" of belief or spiritual conviction—far from it!—but the "otherness" of a personality one couldn't overlook, who commanded one's attention, fascination, at times surprise, and bewilderment from the moment he was seen or heard.

What words come to mind when thinking of Paul Martin? People often say, "unique"; and though the word can be overused, it certainly has more than its usual significance when applied to Paul. Others say "uninhibited"; still others, not content with the one word, say "totally uninhibited." I've heard these and many other phrases to describe the same fact: that in any group which included him—be it platform figures, a church audience, an institute baseball team, an after-church social gathering of young adults, or a luncheon of Christian businessmen—there was always, it seemed, the group *and one other*—the irrepressible Paul Martin.

It was a trait that in his case was entirely natural, entirely free of premeditation or artifice. He even tried to suppress it from time to time, because of occasional misunderstandings or the cautious advice of more conservative pastors and friends. But he couldn't change himself anymore than some could become unnaturally humorous. It was the naturalness of this trait that made it so appealing—and so disastrous to imitate!

All of his life he stood out—whether he wanted to or not! Imagine a funeral procession of cars, all in black or subdued colors, and in the middle of it there is one bright-red Pontiac. Which car would be Paul's? The red Pontiac was, in fact, his; and he did drive it through a funeral procession at Forest Lawn in southern California in the 1940s, not to attract attention but because he hadn't thought about the etiquette of the situation.

Or imagine a photograph taken at a Nazarene campground during a camp meeting. Four ministers are posing before a camera one afternoon during the recreation time. Three are dressed to a T, casual yet impeccable, looking earnestly at the camera. One is in baggy pants, an old brown coat, face and arms dusty, hair matted down, smiling widely—somewhat like a Little Leaguer who has just hit his first home run. Which is Paul Martin? You guessed it, and probably he had just come from one of the afternoon games. The slide was taken at the Northern California camp in the late 50s.

Or take early Saturday morning at an institute. Everyone is trying to sleep. The workers are worn-out from trying to get the kids to bed by the required hour the night before. There are a few hours left before the first breakfast bell rings. From somewhere in the distance you hear the clatter of garbage cans and a trumpet. And the noise doesn't stop but grows. It moves all over the campground and now appears to be headed for your cabin. Soon the door bursts open, and in comes a man with an army hat or a kitchen pot on his head and a whole parade of youngsters behind him! Who would do a thing like that? Paul Skiles knows who would, for he was paid just such a visit at the Northern California camp. Nor was he the only one. Nor was this the last time Paul organized such a 5 a.m. Saturday morning parade.

I walked into a classroom where I was teaching music at the University of California, Berkeley, in the late 60s. As I looked over the class, I noticed a very familiar, beaming face near the back of the room—a face much older than the others. Here was an unannounced student for the day —quiet, respectful, yet somehow the object of most everyone's attention. A visiting professor of music? A pianist who would perform later for the class? Few would have realized the truth: Here was a holiness preacher come to hear his son speak on Beethoven!

And at Paul Martin's funeral, the pastor in charge was reading the names of those who had sent telegrams. "We also received one from Rev. and Mrs. Paul Martin —excuse me, from Rev. and Mrs. Paul Mangum," he said. This pastor, an exceptionally conscientious and able man, was no doubt embarrassed; but Ted leaned over to me and said, "That's just like Paul—he was bound to make an appearance somehow!"

Even his voice had its own special quality—the "gravel baritone" sound, as he so often described it. It changed a good deal from the early years. He never learned to speak "correctly" like an actor, to project without straining. The result was that in his second period of evangelism, in 1953 or '54, he began to lose his voice. This happened in Nampa, Ida., when Eugene Stowe was pastor at the College Church there. In the middle of a strong sermon, the voice began to go, and my relatives and I wondered if he would make it to the end. Soon after, at the Bresee Church in Pasadena, he consulted with some throat specialists and had his vocal cords scraped.

He was required to take a month's rest (this was probably the longest vacation he ever took until his heart attack.) The Bresee Church came through in a wonderful, unexpected way, with an offering of $800 for the week— a sizeable amount in the 1950s—and this income allowed us to spend a month in a motel near Newport Beach, Calif. The time was not without its inconveniences for Paul, for he was ordered by the doctors not to speak *a word for the whole month!* Anyone who knows and remembers Paul Martin knows what a burden *that* was! But he followed instructions, carried a pad of paper around with him, and wrote down his remarks or whispered them softly.

His voice never had another breakdown, but it was never quite the same, either. I was shocked when I listened to the old Porterville radio tapes many years after they were made, to hear the mellow, smooth voice he had in his 30s. In a way, I liked the later quality. It sounded like a voice that had been "over the road" a good deal, not polished or streamlined—much like his character. It seemed to reflect the heavy speaking program he carried on—work that, as he described to Dr. Lawlor, was "fit only for men of iron lungs and leather throats."

There are a few people who probably think of Paul Martin as the most dedicated evangelist they ever knew, having seen him dressed in black suit with Bible wandering around the campground or church property the day before the revival meeting! To my knowledge he never arrived a day late for a revival; but there were a number of times when, after a long, cross-country trip with next to no sleep, he arrived at the church or tabernacle ready to preach, only to find that the meeting began the next day. He didn't wish to embarrass anyone or boast of his energy, so he'd say very little—leaving the odd impression of either a very zealous or a very forgetful pulpiteer.

And he could definitely be "one other" on the platform. There was a picture, unfortunately lost, of him sitting in a very ornate, high-backed church chair—more like a bishop's seat in one of the more formal churches. He is well dressed, as always when on the platform. But he is slouched down in the seat, his hands covering his eyes, laughing at some joke or private thought so uninhibitedly and uproariously that the whole picture is a hilarious study in contrast!

I often wondered about the people visiting a church for the first time on the Saturday night of Paul's revival meeting, who happened to arrive late. The first sight they might see would be the guest speaker, at the pulpit, dressed in a conservative business suit, but wearing a bright orange motorcycle helmet several sizes too big! If they weren't scared off in the first few seconds, they would quickly understand the whole context. The helmet was part of Paul's fun night. During the last years, E. H. Land, the successful manufacturer of Land motorcycle helmets and prominent Nazarene layman, sent Paul a box of beautifully designed, expensive helmets, free of charge, to almost every meeting! This uncalled-for generosity was the source of endless fun for Paul, as he gave them away to the boy or girl who brought the most people to the Saturday night service. The kids worked hard all week to get everyone they knew to come and stand up for them, and the result often was an impressive crowd on that night. And the audience got an unusual treat—for no comedian at any time ever looked funnier or more incongruous than the helmeted Paul Martin!

Some people undoubtedly arrived at Paul's services expecting one thing and getting something quite different!

93

Paul used to enjoy telling of the time I sat behind a man who had come with pen and notebook, expecting a point-by-point sermon-lecture on the functions of Sunday school. After 5 to 10 minutes of Paul's special humor and fairly rambling discourses on a number of subjects, I saw the man slowly fold up his notebook and return it to his pocket. Some must have arrived on certain occasions expecting a detailed and scholarly discussion of an Old Testament passage, only to be the recipient of a sermon like "David's Team," based, loosely, on 2 Samuel 23. "It says about Adino the Eznite," Paul would say, "that 'he lift up his spear against eight hundred, whom he slew at one time' . . . and you talk about shish kebab!" No one enjoyed jokes better than Paul himself. And the shocks he gave some in the audience helped in many cases—they jolted the listeners out of their expectations; without knowing it, they were ready to listen with fresh ears.

As might be expected, some spontaneous ideas were tried once and never again. In one service, as he was about to read a psalm for the scripture of the evening, he suddenly decided to have the "selahs" played by the musicians. One theory about the word "selah," he explained to the audience, was that it indicated a pause when a short passage of music was performed. So, why not play the "selahs" tonight? The musicians had not been cued ahead of time and were totally bewildered as to what to play or how long to go on for each selah. The results were not quite what Paul or anyone else—including the musicians—expected!

No one who happened to hear it will forget his own piano playing—as he accompanied himself for such songs as "'Twas Only an Old Pop Bottle," or "Sweet Rosie O'Grady" for the after-church fellowships. On times like this, one wondered if he might have become a successful entertainer, had he not made his decision for Christ. Paul's answer to this question was that he had never turned down anything except his trousers for the next season.

He always worked well with people of a contrasting personality to himself. The "one other" quality was especially a source of amusement and, occasionally, bewilderment—at these times. The meetings that Paul held at Dr. Lawlor's church in Calgary, Alberta, during Paul's first period of evangelism are perfect examples. Dr. Lawlor, possessing perhaps the best and most genuine knowledge of propriety and etiquette in the church, was quite a contrast to Paul—especially at that time.

Paul was always threatening to do something a little irregular. One night he arrived tieless at the meeting at which he was to speak. In answer to Dr. Lawlor's urgent questions, he explained that tonight he was going to speak on holiness, and he never wore a tie when he did so. Not until a few minutes before he went on the platform did he produce a tie from a pocket—to the great relief of Dr. Lawlor and the others. He would arrive just minutes before he and Dr. Lawlor were to go on the air for the radio programs they were doing. One Sunday afternoon, Dr. Lawlor remembers, "Paul in his typically humorous, yet serious, way announced that he could not preach on the second coming of Jesus Christ (which I had advertised extensively) because he had forgotten to bring his white suit, and he never preached on the Second Coming unless he had a white suit."

Dad even worked well with me—and our personalities were quite different—during the times we presented a musical program with commentary. Before introducing me, he always made himself out as an absolute ignoramus in artistic matters (which was not really true). "Until my son told me differently, I always thought a Bach chorale was where Bach kept his horses; and I can see from your reaction that you probably thought the same!"

For a while he and I did a program together, in which he would introduce a classical work, talk about the composer and the composition, and lead into my performance of it. We made a team: I was quiet and formal; he was exuberant. The two parts of the program had little to do with each other. Whether or not people remember the performance side of it, they quite likely remember Paul's uninhibited, unconventional, and immensely entertaining "explanations" of the classical pieces.

There are so many things one could put in this chapter on Paul the Unpredictable, the "one other," they would exhaust the rest of the book. Those who knew him well will have their own personal memories—ones that will be as funny or as special to them as those mentioned here. If this chapter, besides highlighting a few moments, revives in such readers their own cherished memories—humorous or serious—it will have served a good purpose.

But, of course, Paul Martin could be "one other" in a deeper spiritual sense—he could be God's special instrument at important times, when it seemed as though no one else could do quite what he did. Of the many examples I could mention, one of the most appropriate is the incident Dr. Eugene Stowe tells, which took place during the summer of 1976:

> He and I were speakers at the missionary workshop in Glorieta, N.M. He spoke every morning and I spoke in the evenings. God blessed his ministry to our furloughed missionaries, and they laughed and cried and shouted as he preached in his inimitable way. His last assignment was on Friday morning, and he was to open a camp meeting in New York on Saturday night. I urged him to leave immediately and catch the plane that would get him in there in time to get some rest before the strenuous days of camp meeting. Typically, he refused. "Not on your life," he said. "I want to be here tonight to hear you preach." I argued with him in vain.

That night he was there. I felt led to have a Communion service and asked him and Dr. Jerry Johnson to assist me. As I introduced the service, I made mention of the fact that we were setting two places at the Communion table for those who could not be with us in person. The first, of course, was Christ, who is always the Head of the Communion table. The other place was for Armand Doll, our missionary to Mozambique who was then imprisoned in Lourenco Marques.

When Paul distributed the Communion elements, with his typical creative imagination he put a wafer of bread and a cup of juice at Armand Doll's place. Mrs. Stowe noticed this and was tremendously moved by this gesture. After Communion she felt impressed to ask the group to join in special prayer for Armand Doll's release. Hugh Friberg, the other missionary who had been imprisoned with Armand, was present and came forward to lead the group in prayer. That group of 50 missionaries touched the throne of grace on behalf of their imprisoned colleague.

After the prayer time a regular camp meeting spirit prevailed with notes of praise and thanksgiving being sounded. Less than two weeks later the word came that Armand Doll had been released. No one will ever be able to convince that group of missionaries and myself and my wife that this was not triggered by that prayer time which came about because Paul let the Holy Spirit use him to crystallize the need in his own inimitable way. That was the last time we ever saw Paul, but we shall always cherish the memory of one of the best men whom God ever made and whose life has been so beneficial to our family.

Later that year, in November, Dad and I heard Armand Doll speak about his experiences at the Grand Ole Opry House in Nashville—and Dad went up to see him after the service. It could well be that an inspired addition to that Communion service in the form of Paul Martin's spontaneous gesture helped bring about the wonderful conclusion of that missionary's release. Here was Paul—"one other" and at the same time one "in Christ."

97

12

The Worldwide
Nazarene Parsonage

Paul Martin's life seemed to be, in so many ways, one that expanded as he got older—in the depth and variety of his message, in his own reading and writing, and in his increasing exposure to an ever greater variety of peoples and cultures. This last expansion—best seen in the growing scope of his travels—occurred comparatively late in life.

Until the 1960s he was known and heard almost entirely in the United States and Canada, excluding Alaska and Hawaii. It was not until he was 47 that the area of his ministry broadened. The first expansion out of the United States-Canada area occurred soon after he left the Chinese Church, in 1962. It was to the comparatively new state of Alaska. He toured through Anchorage, Juneau, Fairbanks, and Ketchikan. We thought this trip quite a step away from home at the time, since none of us had been that far away before. He sent back letters, innumerable postcards, and tapes describing the country and remarking on the conditions. "Would you believe it?" he said on one tape, "gasoline is *50 cents a gallon!*" He described the beautiful, inspirational trip he made when he drove from Fairbanks to Anchorage, seeing the splendid views of Mount McKinley. He arrived home with caribou sausages, several souvenirs, and a whole year's supply of anecdotes and illustrations. This was the first of several trips to Alaska.

Then, in 1966, he was part of what Paul Orjala called "possibly the largest evangelistic undertaking of the Church of the Nazarene to date." This was the tour of 16 ambassadors to Latin America—a tour that involved 15 campaigns in 11 countries. It was a joint effort on the part of the NYPS and the Department of World Mission. After receiving the invitation to be part of this great enterprise, Paul changed his summer slate to be able to preach in 6 South American countries.

After a briefing in early July, Paul and one of the teams toured, among other places, Barbados; Haiti; Rio de Janeiro, Sao Paulo, and Brasilia, Brazil; Buenos Aires; Lima, Peru; Santiago, Chile; and Kingston, Jamaica. Capable musicians under the direction of Ray Moore and Dr. David Uerkvitz performed and testified; Paul Skiles spoke and performed in 10 of the campaigns; and speakers Sergio Franco, Dr. Ponder Gilliland, Dr. Willard Taylor, and Paul Martin preached.

The crowds in the services were astonishingly large, Paul remembered: 1,000 people in the Buenos Aires Central Church; 12,000 people in the stadium of Port-au-Prince, Haiti; and 327 in the remote area of Chiclayo, Peru, to name but a few places. Paul, encouraged and challenged by this response, threw himself into his task with unusual enthusiasm, even for him. In spite of the heat, he marched in a Nazarene parade down the streets of Port-au-Prince, Haiti, as energetic, or even more so, as the youngest of the ambassadors, according to Dr. Uerkvitz, who was with Paul much of the time throughout the tour.

As was mentioned before, he had grown accustomed
to interpreters through his work in the Chinese Church,
so that he was able right away to speak with considerable
ease and effectiveness. Each place he would find out how
to best express the jokes and illustrations he wanted to
use. "How shall we put this?" he would ask Dr. Uerkvitz.
"'You don't have to look like you've been baptized in
lemon juice'? or vinegar? Or is there some other sour liquid
they're more familiar with here?"

Due to his and the other workers' effective ministry,
the tour was a wonderful success and a real step forward
in the spreading of the gospel. Paul Orjala writes in the
October 26 issue of the *Herald* in 1966:

> In Port-au-Prince, Haiti, Paul Martin, Paul Skiles,
> and I walked through the stadium with Joseph Simon,
> the national pastor who served as the local coordinator.
> We wondered what would happen that night in the
> first service of four in this large stadium which could
> hold a capacity crowd of more than 17,000. Were we
> attempting too much?
>
> That night we got our answer when 200 seekers
> (120 of them first-time converts) poured out of the
> stands onto the playing field. The swamped counselors
> had to deal with *groups* of seekers rather than indi-
> viduals, as had been the plan. The first night crowd
> of 10,000 grew to more than 12,000 by the last night in
> the stadium, when more than 500 persons found the
> Lord for the first time.

The tour was not without its unforgettable moments
in another sense! One time that Paul, Dr. Uerkvitz, and
the ambassadors of their group would never forget was
their train ride into a suburb of Rio during rush hour.
They were to meet a missionary that evening, so they
took a commuter train at the busiest time of the afternoon.
Never in their lives did they have an experience quite
like it! They were crammed into the train so tightly
they held their arms over their heads, holding onto

nothing, yet unable to move or even fall. A trombone was accidentally released by one of the ambassadors and literally slid down the car on top of the heads of the people. Truly a "sliding trombone"! Dr. Uerkvitz called in Spanish down the length of the car, and the trombone was pushed back up to them.

Getting out at the right stop, during the short 30-second interval that the subway doors were open, was a real physical feat. Dr. Uerkvitz was pushing Paul towards the door with the trombone—and they both had to grab both sides of the door with all their strength and pull themselves out past the multitudes trying to push their way in. All emerged from the train almost in shock—clothes and hair in disarray, buttons torn off. It was an unforgettable introduction to an area of the world far more populated than what most of us—including Paul—are used to.

Later that year, Paul was invited to narrate part of the film that was made on the South American tour. He flew back to Kansas City for three days to provide some of the spoken continuity for the film. He returned optimistic about the film's message, concerned that he had done a good enough speaking job, since his voice was not the usual narrator's voice, and amused at the number of times he had had to say, "Our nets were full too!" relating a certain local fishing event to the whole evangelical endeavor. It was an important phrase, which deserved all the rehearsal, for seldom have Nazarene nets been any fuller than on this tour of which Paul was privileged to be a part.

Then, in 1969, he was asked by the Youth and Communications departments to be part of one of the teams touring Europe that summer. Again, it was an extensive and well-prepared campaign that lasted for several months. Monica took the opportunity to arrange a tour of her own, through American Express, so that she might be with Paul part of the time before and after the campaign proper. The result was they they spent together one of the rare and most enjoyable vacations of their lives, aboard the S.S. *France*—one whole week traveling by boat to Europe without interruptions, people to see, obligations to meet, or places to drive to. One would have had to be part of their incredibly busy schedule to know what a special time this was for them both.

In Amsterdam, 1969

When they arrived in England, Paul still had a few days before his work began; the American Express Company allowed him to be with Monica for the first week of the tour, at no additional expense. He wrote many postcards to me, describing his exhilaration and feeling of adventure as he toured St. Paul's, Windsor Castle, and Buckingham Palace, and as he rode all over town on the elaborate "tube" system of London.

Then it was back to his work. This time it included the special privilege of preaching to the audiences of Glasgow, Scotland; Dublin, Ireland; Haarlem, Holland; Buesingen, Germany; Rome, Florence, and Naples, Italy. He got to see the work of so many dedicated Nazarene missionaries over the years and to add his own part in the spread of the gospel. The work required its own challenges —for Europe is a complex mixture of cultures and traditions, of formal Christian ritual and intricate political climates. He met these challenges with characteristic energy, and he and the ambassadors he toured with grew to be accepted and loved by many.

His second trip to Europe was in November, 1972. I traveled with him on this tour, since I was already in England. The first stop was Berchtesgaden, Germany, for the servicemen's retreat. From our hotel room we could see the magnificent Bavarian Alps, snow-covered and golden in the morning sun. The General Walker Hotel of the retreat is a reconstruction of the old Platterhof, guest quarters for those visiting Hitler during the 40s. In fact, the whole area was filled with National Socialist remains: old bunkers, air raid shelters, the sites of homes since destroyed—Hitler's, Goering's, Bormann's, and Speer's houses. High on the mountain in back still stands the Eagle's Nest, Hitler's teahouse built for him by Bormann on the occasion of the fuehrer's 50th birthday.

This setting—this reminder of totalitarianism and the

denial of Christian values—was now the scene of a beautiful retreat for our Nazarene servicemen. The atmosphere seemed unusually congenial for the meeting, and I have seldom heard Dad speak so well. Paul Skiles and his wife gave an inspirational musical slide program, and Dad followed it with a 15- to 20-minute message. Many recommitted their lives to Christ. Those who were experiencing problems in adjusting to military life and in retaining a firm Christian stand were helped through the week.

From there we went to Italy with then District Superintendent Roy Fuller. We toured through Turin, Florence, and Rome. The response at each place was good—Dad speaking freely through the interpreters he had grown accustomed to using. He had an interesting way of working with interpreters: He would often overlap with their translation, keeping the flow of words going, in an attempt to preserve the emotional impact of his thoughts. When the interpreters grew accustomed to this, the total result was effective and rarely boring.

One incident in Milan, our first overnight stop in Italy, comes to mind, when thinking about Dad's abilities to communicate with almost everyone. We had the early morning free, before catching the train to Turin in time for the meeting that evening. So we walked around in downtown Milan, finally ending up at the magnificent cathedral. Time passed quickly and before we knew it, we had almost no time to get back to the train station. All the taxis were full on the busy streets, and I had no idea what to do.

Dad was out in the middle of the street flagging down every taxi that came by, full or not. Finally, unbelievably, one stopped. We jumped in and the driver asked where we were going—in Italian, of course. He spoke no English; we spoke no Italian. I was trying all the words for *station* I knew—in French, German, and a variety of inflections, most of which are not found in any language or dialect! He drew a blank on every one of them. Finally, Dad struck out his hand, moved it forward in regular jerks, and said, "Choo-choo-choo!" The taxi driver laughed uproariously, and we roared away at great speed, around and between cars, towards the station.

Then it was back to Buesingen, Germany, home of the European Nazarene Bible College. Dad was with the Dr. Ralph Earles, who were there for that year, and saw a number of the converts and future ministers—the results of the years of missionary work on the part of the church. "I can see your footsteps everywhere," he wrote Jerald Johnson, who had done such an important work in Germany in the years before.

In January of 1974 he made another trip to a new area for him—Guam. He was invited there by District Superintendent Virgil Grover to minister to the preachers and the Nazarene schoolteachers and their families affiliated with the U.S. military bases there. Later in the summer

Paul and Monica returning home after the 1969 European tour.

105

of the same year he visited the only state in the Union he had not yet been to: Hawaii. He was the speaker in the district youth camp on Oahu Island and held a revival meeting at the First Church in Honolulu. He also got to visit his sister Mary's children, Ginger and Pat Kaopuiki, who had moved to Hawaii several years before and who were now married and raising families.

In a sense, these trips abroad never stopped; for, in 1976-77—just a matter of weeks before his death—he was busy getting briefed and taking vaccinations for a trip to South Africa and Swaziland. He was to speak to the missionaries there and play an active role in the conferences, services, and rallies planned in those countries.

This continuous expansion of Paul Martin's "parsonage" to finally include so much of the world was an indication of his ability to relate to almost anyone of any culture, land, or generation. It was a rare ability—at once an encouraging indication of the bonds that tie humanity together, in spite of so many differences, and the power of the gospel to reach such diverse peoples. In this case, the instrument of the gospel was a man whose kindness, tolerance, humor, and compassion allowed him to speak a universal language.

13

The Last Years

In 1971, Paul had his first heart attack. For years electrocardiograms had indicated an irregularity in the heartbeat pattern. He was overweight most of his life—a fact which he joked about often. And in the last few years before the attack, he was getting angina pains. So there were plenty of warnings. But it was hard for him to slow down and follow a more cautious life-style. That summer he did what he always had done—exercised vigorously on the sports fields of the camps and institutes, after a largely sedentary year. This abuse finally caught up with him, and he had an attack in a midwestern camp.

Ironically, he was about to take one of those rare vacations. He and Mother were meeting me and my wife in New York City. We were going to depart for a month's tour of Europe, before I settled in London to continue my musical studies. Although the heart attack occurred in the Midwest, Father wasn't really aware of the seriousness of the condition until the second evening in Manhattan. By then the nightly pains had grown too severe, and he couldn't ignore them any longer. His condition was diagnosed at a New York hospital in midtown Manhattan, which was to be his home for the next month. Although it was a "moderate" attack, with good prospects for recovery, the rest of the family cancelled the trip and spent that month in New York City, visiting him every day.

In a sense, it was his first real bout with sickness since the early polio experience. He had a strong constitution and rarely got anything worse than the average cold. In spite of his hyperactive life and constant exposure to people's communicable diseases, meetings were never cancelled for reasons of health. Sometimes when sickness strikes after such a long period of grace, a person tends to be depressed and have trouble coping with the new conditions. Not so much Dad. He had his moments of depression, but he got over them with amazing speed. He read constantly, watched television, and sent innumerable letters to relatives and close friends. Every afternoon his family visited him, showing him cards and Polaroid pictures of the areas of New York they had seen that day.

Before long, he was taking short steps away from the bed, a few more each day. When he reached the window of the hospital room and saw the view of the East River, the sheer beauty of the world struck him in a fresh way; and he realized, as he told us later that day, how much we take that beauty for granted. Before long, he was walking down the hill to the solarium, where he made his first phone call to our hotel. After his release from the hospital, he stayed a few more days in Manhattan, then moved with his family to Ocean City, N.J., to rest and diet for another month. I flew on to London, starting my two-year scholarship abroad.

What was he to do now? He could go into semiretirement, or settle into one of the quieter pastorates, or continue his work on a limited basis. All these would have been justified solutions to the problem of a chronic heart condition. But that wasn't Paul. His call to evangelism was still firm, his sense of mission as strong as ever. He may, indeed, have been influenced by other members of the family. His father-in-law, who had suffered from the same condition, never eased up. His mother, still preaching in a whisper for 10 minutes, still holding revival meetings, fought off cancer and heart disease until 30 days before her death. Even in the last month she dictated her autobiography, *Miracles in White*.

Dad was eager to demonstrate that this recent obstacle was not going to impede him in any way. For quite a while, he didn't even let many people, including near relatives, know about his condition. After the minimum time of convalescence, he and Mother were back on the road, following the slate as scheduled. It was too soon; the angina pains returned, and he was forced to take another rest. This time it was at the home of Dr. Leon Gilbert, who was to remain Dad's doctor and close friend throughout the next years.

Then he was back on the road, full-time, not sparing himself a bit. If anything, he worked harder and preached more vigorously than before, to dispel any doubts as to his ability to continue or his possible slowing down. He carried the nitroglycerin tablets in a "ball-point pen" container and would often take one or two before preaching. I was a bit frightened when I first saw him preach after this illness. He was exhorting as strongly as he had decades before, covering the platform, emphasizing his points with strong gestures. Whatever the medical advisability of this vigorous return, it certainly worked psychological wonders on himself and his audience. I think people quickly forgot he had ever been ill.

My first experience being with Dad after his heart attack and recovery was in London at the start of his second European tour. I met him at Heathrow Airport in

London. His great vigor surprised me. In all senses except literal age he was a young man. The attack had not curbed his energy in the slightest. He arrived with two or three newspapers and all kinds of luggage. And the luggage grew as time went on. I was determined to keep him from lifting things, to treat him as a semi-invalid. It was impossible. As soon as I looked the other way, he would be hauling things from one station to another, one car or taxi to another. Our only disagreement on that European tour occurred when he asked me not to do so much for him.

The five-and-a-half-year period between the first heart attack and his death was one of his most productive periods. It included the publication of two books, *Have a Good Day!* and *Family Fare;* the second trip to Europe; his participation in the 1976 General Assembly—the "family evening" which many remember; a full evangelistic slate; and, a recent development, his interest and involvement in the communications side of the church's work.

The Department of Communications was planning a half-hour television program based on the 1976 General Assembly, later to be called "Let It Happen." The coverage of the assembly had been excellent; what was needed was a narrator to introduce the program and provide the transitions from one episode to the next. Various people were considered. When the professional television technician saw the films of Dad participating in the assembly, his first choice was Paul Martin. This outside opinion confirmed the feeling of many others, and Dad became the master of ceremonies for this, the most successful Nazarene television program up to that time.

Paul became a kind of traveling representative for the Department of Communications, taking with him on his travels a large videotape machine, a copy of "Let It Happen" and "My Little Corner of the World," as well as cassette tapes of the "Showers of Blessing" programs and examples of the 30-second and one-minute radio and television spots for the Church of the Nazarene. At each meeting, he would try to arrange a gathering of local ministers for a showing of "Let It Happen" and a demonstration of the other materials. He would also contact as many local stations as he could, often receiving positive responses because of his warm, unpressured style of presentation. As a result, he played an important part in the church's increasing desire to use television in promoting the spread of the gospel and generating an interest in the local churches. He sent weekly reports back to the Department of Communications, telling of the obstacles overcome, the progress made, and the goals of each pastor. The department, on its side, would respond to each pastoral request for information or materials.

He enjoyed this work for several reasons. It put him in contact with a world he was familiar with—that of radio and television. He saw the media as a means to boost, rather than supplant, the activities of the local church—a philosophy which fit into his general concept of evangelism and his own emphasis in revival meetings. It also gave him a reason to keep up contact with the Department of Communications and the many friends he had there, as well as the general work at the church's headquarters. In a sense, it helped reinforce in him the feeling that he was working for an overall unifying cause, above the diversities of each week. And, like his widening travels, this was an expansion of his area of ministry and witness.

By 1976, his heart condition had worsened somewhat. A second irregularity in the heartbeat had been discovered. The doctors who examined him were increasingly concerned. Paul was worried, though not, apparently, to the extent he should have been. He was never "self-de-

111

Preaching in New York state camp meeting. (Courtesy of James Blandin, Basking Ridge, N.J.)

structive"; he took his medicines faithfully, always rested, and allowed Mother or me to do the main part of the driving. He declined several positions, including one connected with a large church which would have allowed him to reduce the hectic pace. He did not feel ready to slow down.

I had the opportunity to travel with him the last months of his life. Those days will always be with me: the times of fun and prayer; the privilege of hearing a person whose message was always fresh, whose vitality never diminished. The sights we saw—from the top of Pikes Peak to the Gulf Coast of Florida, from the sunrise over the Grand Canyon to evenings near the Blue Mountains of Idaho—these sights did not surpass the joy in being with a person so filled with humor and joy, so deeply involved in his mission, so in love with the work to which he had dedicated his life.

112

He spent that last Christmas with his family in Berkeley. Soon after, he was in Washington State for a meeting, and he saw again the little town of Mukilteo—the site of so many rich experiences and memories for him. Then a meeting in Moscow, Ida., and then back to Oakland.

We were about to depart for a tour of Africa when, as Dr. Zachary said, "God invited him to a greater tour of the eternal city." On January 13, 1977, after a day spent with his family, he died in his sleep of another heart attack. The funeral service was given at First Church of the Nazarene in Oakland. Gilbert Rushford, who had worked with him often at the Beulah Park Camp Meeting in California, sang; Dr. Zachary, his district superintendent and good friend, gave a warm appreciation; and Dr. Lawlor, who had been an inspiration to Paul and Monica over the years, gave the message.

It was a life that never declined but always grew, to the very end. His parish encompassed first his immediate family, then the churches he pastored and preached in, and finally the entire Church of the Nazarene at home and abroad. It became his larger family, his larger parish. I think it fitting, therefore, to end this story of his life not with his death, but with a short section, in his own words, of a service he gave throughout the country, during the last years of his ministry—an inspirational moment one might call "The Family Altar." It sums up, in many ways, the guiding principles of his life and the overriding themes of his message.

14

The Family Altar

A Message by Paul Martin

At the front of this church is an altar. Oh, I love the altar! It's not really a place for furniture or flowers. There are no statues here. What is it, Rev. Martin? Well, it's a place to kneel, a place to pray. It's the sweetest place in the church. I love the altar.

It's here that we dedicate babies. Organist, would you play "Jesus Loves Me, This I Know"? Oh, I've held many babies—so wrapped up in their father's baptismal gown I wasn't sure I had them right side up or not! I held my own son. My dad, a Nazarene preacher, prayed for God to help my boy and help his father. How many of you ever brought a child to this altar, or one like this, for dedication—it makes the altar precious to you—would you slip your hand up? I hope you bring some more! Hope some of you bring at least one!

We marry couples at the altar. Organist, play a little of "The Wedding March." No, I'm not going to marry anyone now, though my summer rates are still on! I was getting ready to marry a couple one time, and the bride cried all the way down the aisle. I can't stand any tension, so I whispered to her, "I don't know why you're crying—maybe you know this fellow better than I do!" And she stopped crying! How many people in this audience were married in this church, or one like this, would you raise your hand? That's great—and still together! It makes the altar a wonderful place for you.

Of course I love the altar because we've laid to rest those we've loved and lost. "Abide with Me, Fast Falls the Eventide"—would you play some of that? My father was laid to rest at the altar of the College Church at Red Deer, Alberta—he was president of Canadian Nazarene College. Mother, at the altar of the Portland, Ore., First Church. You have memories too, this morning. How many of you, in this church or some humble holiness church like this, have had a memorial service for someone you love, and that makes the altar special to you too, would you raise your hand with me? God bless you. It's a precious place.

But I love the altar, for, you see, this is where we find peace and salvation. It's like kneeling at "The Old Rugged Cross." How many of you ever came to this altar, or one like it, and by coming found Christ and peace, would you raise your hands? I see them! Oh, I see them! God bless you. It is a place of victory, a place to pray, a place to find Jesus! This altar is so fixed that tears will not stain it. And it's strong enough to hold you and your burdens.

*   *   *

I want you to join me in a closing moment, a moment in which to search our hearts. You see, I want us to get together as families, all over this auditorium. Young people, find your parents. Choir, why don't you come down and meet with your family? I want my family to come up front. Are there any college people, singles, or grade school children who are here all by yourselves this morning?

115

Come stand over by the organ. None of you are visitors today—we're just one big family.

Please bow your heads. As we sing, before the pastor prays, I want to invite you to do two things. First, I want someone in every family group to talk it over with the family. I really do. Mother, talk it over with the family. Dad, talk it over. Talk to each one. Ask them if it's all right; ask them if they ought to pray. Ask them if they would, this day, make a choice for Christ. I want to talk to my family. I want to talk to those who are here by themselves today. Second, if there is someone in this audience who means as much to you as your family—someone who needs to pray—just slip over and invite him to come to the altar for prayer. If members of your family come, I would like the whole family to come with them.

Listen to me: If our church fails, it will be at the family level—it will be in our homes. Let's do something about it today! Make a decision that it will be just a whole lot different in your family: a new family altar; a lot more prayer; a lot more concern for holy living.

While the pastor prays, you pray. Make promises, will you? Make decisions. And when the prayer is over, the service will be ended.

I will remain at the altar. If there are those who, rather than leave the building, would wish to come forward to talk it over, to pray, or ask me to remember you in prayer, I will still be here.